THE HOMESTEAD
STEEL STRIKE
of 1892

THE HOMESTEAD
STEEL STRIKE
of 1892

Nancy Whitelaw

MORGAN
REYNOLDS
PUBLISHING
Greensboro, North Carolina

american workers

The Homestead Steel Strike of 1892

The Pullman Strike of 1894

The Ludlow Massacre of 1913-14

Mother Jones

THE HOMESTEAD STEEL STRIKE OF 1892

Copyright © 2006 by Nancy Whitelaw

Library of Congress Cataloging-in-Publication Data

Whitelaw, Nancy.
    The Homestead Steel Strike of 1892 / Nancy Whitelaw.— 1st ed.
        p. cm.
    Includes bibliographical references and index.
    ISBN-13: 978-1-931798-88-4 (library binding)
    ISBN-10: 1-931798-88-5 (library binding)
    1. Homestead Strike, Homestead, Pa., 1892. 2. Steel industry and
trade—United States—History. 3. Carnegie, Andrew, 1835-1919. 4. Carnegie
Steel Company—History. I. Title.
    HD5325.I51892 .W48 2006
    331.89'04691420974885—dc22
                                                2005027113

Printed in the United States of America
First Edition

*To Kathy and Patty, with love and thanks
for all you have done for me*

CONTENTS

The Homestead Strike. (Courtesy of the Granger Collection.)

1.
American Dreams

On July 5, 1892, a wary group of lawmen climbed off a train in Homestead, Pennsylvania. Deputy Sheriff Samuel Cluely and nine others had been sent from nearby Pittsburgh to protect the facilities of Homestead Steel Works, the huge mill owned by the Carnegie Steel Company. The president of the company, and principal owner Andrew Carnegie's right-hand man, Henry C. Frick, had locked out all of Homestead's 3,800 employees a few days before and was refusing to meet with the leaders of the union that represented the skilled workers. Tensions were rising as the workers and towns-people who depended on the mill for their livelihood grew increasingly frustrated. Frick had contacted the local sheriff and claimed to be afraid the angry workers would vandalize the mill. He insisted the sheriff provide

The mill town of Homestead, Pennsylvania, is located just upriver from Pittsburgh. Beginning in the early nineteenth century, Pittsburgh's proximity to large coal deposits and excellent positioning along major trade routes made it one of the world's leading industrial powerhouses. (Library of Congress)

deputies to protect it, or he would call in private security.

Although the workers had made no move toward damaging the mill, the sheriff had no choice but to send his men into the volatile situation. When Cluely and the other nervous deputies disembarked from the train at Homestead, they were met by an armed and angry crowd of 2,000 men. Cluely, determined to do his duty, took a legal notice from his pocket and read it to the crowd. The notice authorized him and his men to make sure anyone who attempted to show up for work at the mill was not harmed—in other words, to provide protection for the strikebreakers, referred to as "scabs" by the union—and to protect the works from vandalism. He then stated, "Our instructions are to proceed to the Homestead Steel Works with all possible speed."

As soon as Cluely finished his statement, one of the workers shouted, "You fellows will never get to the gates [of the mill] alive." The crowd broke into cheers.

Cluely quickly realized that to proceed with his instructions would probably lead to violence. Wisely, when a leader of the armed protesters offered him safe passage back to Pittsburgh, he took it. Before he left, however, Cluely warned the workers that the fight was not over. More men would be returning, he said, and they would come armed.

What Cluely did not know was that reinforcements were already on their way. Henry Frick was a savvy man. He probably knew the deputies would be turned away, but before he called in private guards he had to make a show of allowing official law enforcement the opportunity to surround the steel mill. He must have known that nine deputies would not have a chance against 2,000 armed and angry locked-out workers.

LOCKOUTS VERSUS STRIKES

The terms lockout and strike are often used to refer to the same thing, although they are technically different. A lockout occurs when an employer prevents employees from working; a strike is when employees stop work of their own volition. Most strikes entail a walkout, but until they were made illegal in 1939, sit-down strikes (in which people did not work but did not leave the premises, either) were often used because they could prevent employers from resuming production with replacement workers.

The private guards Frick had hired were from the Pinkerton National Detective Agency, which earned most of its money busting up strikes. No single group was hated by organized labor more than the Pinkerton Agency, which was suspected of murder and perjury in other battles between workers and owners. The arrival of Pinkertons in Homestead would set off a gunfight that would become one of the most bloody and dramatic episodes in the long conflict between labor and management. The Homestead Strike, the events which led to it, and its aftermath, is a watershed in the history of American capitalism.

The great Industrial Revolution that transformed the United States in the second half of the nineteenth century was built on, and of, steel. By the 1870s, steel had replaced iron as the primary material in the new ships, factories, and office buildings going up in New York, Chicago, San Francisco, and other fast-growing cities.

It was railroad construction, however, that consumed the majority of the steel in these early years. Before the Civil War, most tracks and bridges were made of iron. But iron was not as durable as steel; it wore out quickly and cracked easily. Trains derailed and bridges collapsed because of faulty rails or beams.

Steel, an alloy of iron and carbon, is stronger and more durable. It had first been produced in the fifteenth century, but steel production required prepared pig iron (raw, unprocessed iron) to be heated to over 1000°F in order to cook out the impurities, including sulfur and phosphorous. The high cost of heating the iron made steel prohibitively expensive. This changed in 1855 when Englishman Henry Bessemer patented a new process.

The Bessemer converter was a pear-shaped container with an opening at the top, usually constructed so it could be tilted to pour out the "cooked" steel. The Bessemer process was relatively simple, but dangerous. Once the pig iron had been heated well over 1000°F, air was blown into the pear-shaped container from the bottom, setting off a volcanic reaction that sent a flame blasting from the top of the converter for several minutes. This blue-hot flame burned off impurities, and what was left was molten steel, ready for cooling and shaping.

The Bessemer converter made it much less expensive to manufacture steel. Wily entrepreneurs, such as Andrew Carnegie, were quick to realize that steel could now replace iron in general use. Carnegie saw the Bessemer converter on a trip to England, hurried back to Pennsylvania, arranged for financial backing, licensed the process from Bessemer, and plunged into the steel business.

The Bessemer converter only worked with pig iron that had a low phosphorous and sulfur content. A few years later, a slower-working, open-hearth process was developed that produced a high-quality steel from a lower-quality iron. The slower method could also reheat steel scraps left over from the fabrication process, which cut down on waste and reduced production costs.

Steel workers tend a furnace that uses the open-hearth method that Carnegie would later implement. (Library of Congress)

Carnegie eventually introduced the open-hearth method in some of his plants, including the giant one at Homestead, outside of Pittsburgh. Unlike most of the steel plants in operation in 1892, the Homestead mill was primarily equipped to produce I-beams used in construction instead of materials for railroads.

Although the new steel industry revolutionized engineering and construction, and made some people rich beyond belief, working in the mills was not easy. The conditions inside the steel mill at Homestead were

Opposite: *This drawing of a Bessemer converter at the Homestead Steel Works gives an idea of the stressful conditions under which steel workers labored.* (Courtesy of the Granger Collection.)

described by more than one visitor, and laborer, as resembling the Hell pictured in medieval paintings. The open-hearth method, which Carnegie used extensively, required the pig iron to be heated to 2,500°F, five hundred degrees hotter than the Bessemer process.

Working the Bessemer converters was not easy, either. This process, with its frequent volcanic explosions, was responsible for thousands of accidents and deaths. Even without an accident it was frightening. One visitor to Homestead recorded his observations:

> The powerful jets of air sprang upward through the mass of metal. The air expanding in volume divides itself into globules, or bursts violently upward, carrying with it some hundredweight of fluid metal which again falls into the boiling mass below. Every part of the apparatus trembles under the violent agitation.

A common type of mishap, often fatal, occurred when a converter full of cooked steel exploded as it was being lifted to pour its contents into a mold. Those below died in a deluge of white-hot molten steel. Another type of frequent steel mill accident became the subject of a grim joke. When a worker fell from a catwalk into a pool of hot steel, he was said to have "created his own mold."

Although specific figures were not kept—because owners did not want the information made public—total accidental deaths in the Homestead works for 1891 were around three hundred. There were over 3,000 serious injuries in Pittsburgh area mills the same year.

In April 1892, one workman described a typical accident in the mill for the *Homestead Local News:*

> When the blast is put on, it forces a terrific blaze containing particles of the molten steel, out against an iron shield. In the course of a few hours there is an accumulation of metal [referred to as "the skull"] on the shield or wall which of course is quite heavy and must be removed at frequent intervals, otherwise it would fall, which it did in this instance. . . . Passing somewhat underneath the shield is a pressure pipe. . . . When the skull fell, it struck the pipe referred to, causing the pressure to escape. Released from control, the vessel containing molten metal tipped over and emptied into the pit below where it came in contact with moisture, resulting in a terrific explosion. The metal was scattered in all directions, some of it striking the opposite wall seventy feet away. It is not surprising that many workmen were burned. Indeed the great wonder is that more were not fatally burned. The list is long enough however.

Even without an accident, working in the mill was miserable. One visitor remembered, "Everywhere in the enormous sheds were pits gaping like the mouth of hell, and ovens emitting a terrible degree of heat, with grimy men filling and lining them." Temperatures near where the steel was cooked could reach over 130°F.

The machines controlled the pace of the work. Some men heated the furnaces; others pulled out the finished ingots (metal shaped in a mold) and sent them onward to the rougher, who shoved them into the roller. There was no time to catch a breath, rest a weary muscle, or even visit the bathroom. The men shaping or cutting the steel had to withstand the incredibly loud, giant rolling machines and the saws that screeched at ear-piercing levels as they cut into the cold steel.

Most of the men worked twelve-hour days, which meant during some of the year they were at work before dawn and left after dusk. The long hours were exhausting, leading to more deadly accidents. Of course, there was no disability or social security for disabled workers or benefits to take care of widows and other survivors.

The town of Homestead had only been founded twenty years before the strike. Before the mill was built, six hundred people lived in the village situated in a sharp bend of the Monongahela River, a few miles upstream from Pittsburgh. By 1892, about 11,000 people lived in Homestead. Almost every able-bodied male worked at the steel mill, which had approximately 3,800 on the payroll.

Homestead was only one of several mills on the river, and the pollution was terrible. The air was always full of smoke and dust; sunlight struggled to pierce the gray and brown haze. Pollutants from the mills and the sewage draining from Homestead and other towns had devastated plant and animal life in the river.

The town of Homestead sat perched on the hill above the steel works. The Monongahela River can be seen in the distance. (Library of Congress)

The town of Homestead ran right up to the mill. The streets were unpaved, and all the buildings were made of wood. Because of the hilly terrain, ramshackle houses were thrown up with little care given to design or urban planning. There were no zoning laws, and the houses were squeezed tightly together. The average lot had only twenty feet of street frontage. The tight confines meant that many of the dwellings never received a ray of natural light, and the tiny yards were muddy year round. The writer Hamlin Garland described the town "as squalid as could well be imagined, and the people were mainly of the discouraged and sullen type to be found everywhere where labor passes into the brutalizing stage of severity."

As miserable as it might have been, the steel mill provided jobs that generally paid more than other industrial jobs, particularly for the skilled men represented by the Amalgamated Association of Iron and Steel Workers (AAISW). Even the unskilled workers who could not join the union benefited from the wages and conditions it negotiated. The mill provided a livelihood and an opportunity for the next generation to live better than the present generation, which was already the core of what came to be called the American Dream. The workers were prepared to fight to preserve their hard-won gains. Unfortunately, they were up against two men who were equally willing to fight. Andrew Carnegie and Henry Frick believed as deeply in the American Dream as the workers did. But their vision of that dream was centered around the right to own private property and the property owner's right to use that property as he wished. These two conflicting versions of the same dream, which are still doing battle in our world today, were at the core of the Homestead tragedy.

2.
One Immigrant's Story

In 1886, after steel mills and other investments in rapidly industrializing America had already made him one of the wealthiest men in the world, Andrew Carnegie wrote an essay in which he said, "The right of the working-man to combine and to form trades-unions is no less sacred that the right of manufacturers to enter into associations and conferences with his fellows, and it must sooner or later be conceded." In another essay published that year, Carnegie proclaimed that strikes and lockouts—when owners shut down operations to avoid negotiating with a union—were inexcusable. Workers had the right to sell their labor to the highest bidder, he said, and owners had to accept that as a basic principle of a free economy. A strike or lockout, he said, was an admission of failure on the part of the owners. Carnegie, who had made much of his fortune by putting together deals, seemed to think that making deals with unions was part of the capitalist's job and to resort to brute force was unjust and inefficient.

The events at Homestead in 1892 pointed out the contradictions, even hypocrisy, between Carnegie's stated views and his actions when his own interests were at stake. But even before the strike at Homestead, Carnegie had shown his true colors. Less than two weeks before Christmas 1884, Carnegie had closed down the Edgar Thompson Steel Mill outside of Pittsburgh with the clear intent to drive out the union. There had been a recent panic in the stock market, brought on by a corruption scandal, which had led to a sharp recession. The price of steel had taken a dive, and when the AAISW and the Knights of Labor, which had made inroads organizing at Edgar Thompson, refused to discuss a wage cut, Carnegie ordered the mill closed.

Carnegie admitted to his lieutenants at Edgar Thompson that the goal of the lockout was to crush the unions, although he publicly claimed it was to have time to install new machinery. The workers, however, were not fooled. Most realized that only nonunion men would be rehired when the works restarted.

When the rehiring began, a new wage scale was announced. Edgar Thompson would also be reinstating twelve-hour days, instead of the eight-hour days that the union had agreed to earlier. In addition, because of the new, more efficient equipment, fewer workers would be

Andrew Carnegie. (Courtesy of the Granger Collection.)

needed. By the end of January 1885, the union was broken. The men who were offered jobs had to sign individual contracts with the company.

This glaring contradiction between what Carnegie

Andrew Carnegie's birth town of Dunfermline, Scotland, was known for its prosperous textile industry. (Library of Congress)

said and what he did might not have been totally cynical on his part. He was clearly a man torn between his driving ambition and his somewhat sentimental attachment to his own humble beginnings. Carnegie was born in 1835 to a family that had long earned their living as weavers. As a young man, Carnegie's father, William, had operated several looms from his home. The development of steam looms, which led to the consolidation of textile manufacturing into an industry with wage workers, drove craftsmen such as William Carnegie out of business. During the early years of Andrew's childhood, his father valiantly tried to hold on in Scotland. Then the family, as so many had before and would in the future, set their sights on crossing the Atlantic and starting again in the fabled land of opportunity.

Andrew was twelve when his family landed in New

York and made their way to a new home in a suburb of Pittsburgh, Pennsylvania. Late in life Carnegie wrote an autobiography that turned the story of his early years into the quintessential American success story. He did indulge in a few embellishments, however, such as claiming his mother mortgaged the family home to raise capital for his first big investment, when Carnegie actually got the money from wealthy acquaintances. But by his death in 1919, the story of how Carnegie rose from poverty to become perhaps the wealthiest man in the world was a testament to his intelligence and determination, and to his skill at snooping out extraordinary opportunities and taking advantage of them.

Though he was a smart child, Carnegie's family could not afford for him to go to school. He had to go to work. His first job, in a textile mill, lasted two years. He hated the hours and the dark and dirty work. At night he attended bookkeeping classes and was finally able to leave the mill for a job delivering messages for a telegraph company. Soon he was one of a handful of people in the country who could transcribe Morse code by ear. He also trained himself to remember the name and face of every prominent businessman he met on his message delivery rounds.

The bright, ambitious Andy Carnegie soon came to the attention of Tom Scott, an executive with the powerful Pennsylvania Railroad. Scott, who would later become president of the railroad and one of Carnegie's biggest benefactors, hired young Carnegie to run the railroad's new telegraph operation. Carnegie used his time with Scott to learn about business and to make contacts.

In 1856, Scott gave Carnegie his first insider investment tip. Carnegie borrowed five hundred dollars and made the investment and was soon rewarded with his first stock dividend check. "It gave me the first penny of revenue from capital—something that I had not worked

The Pennsylvania Railroad, the company in which Carnegie learned much of his early business savvy, provided extensive freight and passenger service throughout the eastern United States. To this day, many of the railroad's grand passenger terminals retain the name "Penn Station." (Library of Congress)

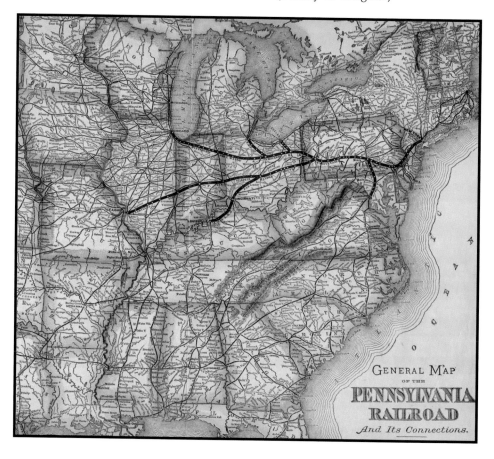

GENERAL MAP
OF THE
PENNSYLVANIA
RAILROAD
And Its Connections.

for with the sweat of my brow. 'Eureka!' I cried. 'Here's the goose that lays the golden eggs,'" he later wrote.

Once he discovered the magic of investing, Carnegie never looked back. He continued working for the railroad for several years, all the while taking advantage of the type of insider tips that could land him in prison today. He became a wealthy man very quickly. By 1863, he was earning nearly $50,000 a year from investments while his railroad salary was only $2,400. But the railroad job was valuable as a source of investment opportunities and contacts to the wealthy and powerful, so he stayed on.

Carnegie soon expanded his stock holdings into bridge building and iron making. He knew that, although the railroads were subject to booms and busts, in the long-term the rapidly expanding U.S. economy was growing ever more dependent on them. Eventually, there would always be a market for rails and other construction materials. It was during this time that he realized steel was a better material than iron, if only there was a cheap way to manufacture it.

The years following the Civil War were marked by rampant corruption, which made investing treacherous and exhausting. Though trading on insider information is illegal today, at the time it was an accepted practice. Carnegie never hesitated to use insider information, but he developed a reputation for honest dealing that became his most valuable asset.

As he neared the age of forty, Carnegie decided to cut

back on his holdings and to retire early. He was wealthy enough to never have to worry about money, and he was weary of hustling from one investment project to another. He had taken several trips to Europe to sell bonds to raise money for railroad and bridge projects and entertained the idea of spending part of the year abroad and the rest in his new mansion in New York City.

There was another alternative, however. Instead of running from one investment to another, he could concentrate on just one. As he put it in his autobiography, he decided the path to true wealth was to "Put all good eggs in one basket and then watch that basket." The problem was coming up with the right investment.

Then, in 1872, Carnegie traveled to Great Britain to raise money for a project. While there he met some British steel manufacturers and made the fateful trip to see Henry Bessemer, the inventor of the Bessemer converter. Carnegie, who was well aware of the problems presented by using iron to make railroad ties and build bridges, instantly realized that steel would be the material of the future. He also knew that the coal indigenous to Pennsylvania was perfect for use in the Bessemer converter. He had found the right investment.

Carnegie licensed the use of the Bessemer process in the United States. When he returned home he began raising money from friends and business connections to build his first steel mill. Shrewdly, he named the Edgar Thompson works, to be located at Braddock Falls outside of Pittsburgh, after a prominent local businessman

British inventor Henry Bessemer patented the groundbreaking Bessemer process, using his Bessemer converter, in 1855. This fast and efficient steel-making process was a development of an ancient Chinese technique.

he hoped would make a major investment. When his first company, Carnegie, McCandless and Company, was founded in 1872, it was the largest steel firm in the area.

Still, the new company got off to a rocky start that might have frightened away a less confident entrepreneur. A deep depression that would haunt the remainder of the decade began in 1873. But Carnegie, McCandless and Company emerged from this trying time not only intact but stronger than most of the competition. Carnegie was determined to hold down costs, and ironically, the bad times made that easier. Other less disciplined companies collapsed, or sold out to Carnegie, for pennies on the dollar.

Carnegie had one constant business mantra: "Mind the costs and the profits will take care of themselves." It was impossible for one firm to control prices, he said, so the emphasis should always be on what could be controlled: expenditures. It was a wise philosophy that others too often ignored—and suffered the consequences. Following this simple advice, Carnegie's company quickly became the predominant steel manufacturer in Pennsylvania. Of course, one of the main costs Carnegie controlled was wages. The depression of 1873 made that easier, as thousands of workers, many of them unskilled immigrants, were out of work.

Carnegie also took advantage of the economic downturn to buy up assets at bargain-basement prices. As he bought equipment, coal mines, and entire companies, he discovered that often the most valuable newly acquired assets were less tangible than land and minerals. Many of the men who played critical roles in his future success, including Henry Frick, came to him in acquisitions. Others were attracted from the railroad and oil business, or from mining companies and banks.

Carnegie acquired the steel works at Homestead in 1883 from the Pittsburgh Bessemer Steel Company. He scooped up the mill at a bargain price due to a temporary downturn in the price of steel—and because of the labor troubles that plagued the plant, which had been organized by the AAISW. Pittsburgh Bessemer had tried to take a tough stance against the union but had been bested, and the company was now willing to let the works go at a loss.

Carnegie knew he was inheriting a tradition of labor troubles when he bought Homestead but did not let that stop him. He would deal with that later. Homestead was a newer plant that he planned to convert from making rails to manufacturing construction steel, particularly I-beams for large buildings. I-beams are a staple in construction and are so-called because of their distinctive shape. The conversion had not been long completed when Henry Clay Frick became company president.

3.
Henry Clay Frick

While Carnegie had written essays extolling the rights of labor, the man he made president of his company, and the man he would eventually leave behind to deal with the conflict at Homestead in 1892, had different feelings. Frick thought unions were illegal and ran contrary to the basic idea of American capitalism—the right of owners to have full control of their property, regardless of the effect it had on workers, the environment, or society in general.

Henry Clay Frick was named after Henry Clay, one of the most important political figures of the early republic. Frick certainly had the ambition to match his namesake, but unlike the senator from Kentucky and four-time presidential candidate Henry Clay, Frick focused his considerable intellect on improving his own situation in life, not solving national problems.

Frick's father was a failed artist, but his grandfather was a successful merchant and whiskey distiller. Grandfather Abraham Overholt paid for Frick's education and then gave him his first job. Frick, who was too impatient to remain in college when there was money to be made, eventually became head bookkeeper in the distillery.

When he was twenty, Frick was offered a chance to enter the coke business. Coke is a necessary ingredient in steel manufacturing. When it is placed into iron ore and heated, coke welds with the impurities in the ore to form slag, which is then removed and discarded. What is left is pure molten iron that can be used to make steel.

Making coke was a time-consuming and expensive process. First, coal was dumped into domed ovens made of brick. The beehive ovens had twelve-foot bases and

Abandoned coke ovens near Pittsburgh, Pennsylvania. (Library of Congress)

Coal mining, which often involved working twelve-hour days underground, was an arduous and sometimes deadly job. In this image, a miner sifts through coal pieces in a Pittsburgh mine. (Library of Congress)

stood seven feet tall. They were usually lined in rows so that trains could pull alongside and dump coal into the openings at the top. The coal was baked for two days and nights, burning off the gases and other impurities. Then what was left, the coke, was washed and pulled from the oven with long rakes.

Not all coal can be turned into coke, but the coal mined in the Pittsburgh area was highly suitable. As he entered the business, Frick already knew one of the keys to success was to become larger and more efficient than his competitors, which meant larger plants and more acquisitions of coal mines. He threw himself into his new business with a combination of a young man's enthusiasm and the shrewdness that was necessary to become a titan of industry during the topsy-turvy early years of industrialization. He shared with Carnegie the talent for focusing on efficiency in production, particularly in holding down labor costs, while also having the fearlessness to borrow large sums of money to buy ever more coal mines and coking ovens. By 1873, Frick controlled the largest coke operation in the area, with over two hundred ovens.

Just as it had for Carnegie, 1873 turned out to be a climactic year for Frick. During the first year of the economic depression, businesses failed almost daily. Those that were poorly managed and had the most debt were the first to go. Frick managed to turn the bad times to his advantage. Because he operated the most efficient coking operation, he was able to make a profit even in bad times. He was also able to buy out many of his competitors. By 1882, when the depression had lifted and coke prices had rebounded, H. C. Frick and Company owned over 3,000 acres of coal-producing land and ran over a thousand coke ovens. At thirty-four, Frick was a multimillionaire.

It seems almost inevitable that the two like-minded men would come together. When he had entered the steel business, Carnegie's original plan had been to produce his own coke. He bought ovens and coal reserves and hired a manager to run them. But he soon discovered that he needed more coke than he could produce himself and that he could probably purchase it for less than it cost him to manufacture. He offered to sell his ovens and mines to Frick.

As Carnegie and Frick negotiated the sale, Carnegie became impressed with the younger businessman, and their talks veered into a different direction. Why not have Frick become the exclusive supplier of coke to Carnegie's mills? Frick would take a half-interest in Carnegie's coke ovens and Carnegie would take a 10 percent interest in H. C. Frick and Company. Carnegie would get a steady supply of coke at prices agreed upon each year; Frick would get guaranteed sales to Pittsburgh's largest steel producer and access to enough capital to expand even further.

As might be expected, however, a partnership between two such driven and shrewd men was inevitably volatile. Frick almost immediately began pressuring Carnegie to finance the purchase of more coal fields. At first Carnegie was resistant but soon saw an opportunity. He began buying up stock in H. C. Frick and Company and Frick used the capital to buy coal fields. Carnegie also secretly bought stock from other investors in Frick's company. Then, in 1884, Frick made the unpleasant discovery that Carnegie now owned 50 percent of the company, while Frick owned only 16 percent. Carnegie held controlling interest.

Frick soon learned that being in a subservient position to Andrew Carnegie was not always pleasant. For one thing, he had lost control of the price he could charge Carnegie for coke. He could raise prices to other

The young Henry Clay Frick. (Library of Congress)

customers if the market would bear it, but Carnegie always got his coke at a bargain. Frick soon grew frustrated with this situation, resigned his position as president of the company, and took an extended European trip.

The two industrialists, however, were held together by mutual need that ran deeper than coke prices. Carnegie admired Frick's astuteness and skill at managing vast operations. They shared a passion for managing costs. Frick was especially good at spotting deals, for which he needed access to Carnegie's vast capital reserves to expand operations and achieve greater economies of scale. The two reconciled and Frick returned to the fold, although he still chafed when Carnegie treated the coke business as the handmaiden to the larger steel concerns.

Frick began to realize that he needed to become more deeply involved in steel. That was where the real action and wealth were. He got his chance to move from coke to steel after Carnegie's brother and right-hand man, Tom, died in 1886. Carnegie offered Frick an opportunity to buy into Carnegie Steel.

Their relationship continued to be turbulent, however. In May 1887, the workers in the coke plants, which had been organized by the Amalgamated Association of Mine Laborers and the Knights of Labor, went on strike demanding higher pay.

Frick wanted to refuse to even talk with the unions. Workers were employed at the owner's pleasure, he insisted. Unions, in Frick's opinion, were illegal organizations, even criminal enterprises, designed to extort money from owners of businesses.

Carnegie saw a bigger picture. Not only did he maintain a sentimental attachment to the worker, but he was also more interested in having coke for his steel business than in standing down the unions. He demanded that Frick meet with the union leaders to negotiate a compromise on the wage issue. Instead, Frick resigned his position as president of H.C. Frick and Company and took yet another extended trip to Europe.

Carnegie soon realized his mistake. He needed Frick at his side; he had grown dependent on his managerial skill. It took the two stubborn men all summer and part of the fall to reconcile. In November 1887, they finally met at Carnegie's Scottish castle, and Carnegie welcomed Frick back. But this time, Frick would not merely be running the coke operation. Henry Clay Frick was named president of Carnegie Brothers and Company with an 11 percent interest. The two titans of industry had finalized a partnership that would weld them together in one of the bloodiest and most controversial conflicts in the history of American capitalism.

4.

Labor Rising

The AAISW, which represented most of the skilled workers at Homestead, had been formed in 1876 from three other unions: the United Sons of Vulcan from Pittsburgh, the Associated Brotherhood of Iron and Steel Heaters, Rollers, and Roughers of the United States, and the Iron and Steel Hand's Union, both from Chicago. Just as the recession years of the 1870s had forced consolidation in the steel industry, it had also pushed these three smaller unions together into a comprehensive and cohesive union that represented skilled workers at several steel and iron companies.

Unions, in which workers bond together to present a united front when dealing with business owners and management and negotiating for better wages and working conditions, had grown up along side the new industrial enterprises. In a country dedicated to the ideal that individual achievement was the key to material success, the idea of workers bonding together to form unions was controversial from the beginning. In most parts of Europe there had long existed a social system that divided the population into different classes. In the United States during the nineteenth century, a counter ideology had developed that promised easier social mobility, determined by an individual's talent and willingness to work hard. It was this faith in the American meritocracy that attracted many immigrants, such as Andrew Carnegie's family, to the United States.

The rise of huge industries in the post-Civil War period put this meritocratic ideal to a test. How were thousands of workers, required to work twelve-hour days in horrible conditions, with little control over their time or environment, to take charge of their lives and move up the social ladder, regardless of how determined or talented they might be? Maybe the solution was for workers to band together into a union, and to use the strength of many to demand better opportunity for all. As manufacturers grew more powerful, and the government became more and more focused on serving the interests of business, many workers decided the only way they could be heard was to form a union.

The question of the proper relationship between the employee and the employer had arguably been the most central question to the U.S. economy from the

The late nineteenth century saw the metamorphosis of many rural American towns into booming industrial centers. (Library of Congress)

beginning. It took a bloody Civil War to determine if there was a role for slave labor in the United States. But the war had done nothing to determine what the proper relationship should be between management and the vast majority of Americans who had to work for them. Furthermore, what was the role of government in the economy?

In the years immediately after the Civil War, many leaders of the nascent labor movement, particularly those who grabbed the attention of the public and the authorities, were inspired by the more radical ideas of socialism and communism that were gaining prestige in Europe at the same time. Socialists believed that the root of economic injustice was private property. As long as a small number of people could accumulate vast wealth and exert the power of life and death over many, there would be injustice. The only solution was an end to private property and its replacement with a system that guaranteed everyone an equal share of the wealth that was produced. A more radical idea that gained some currency was anarchy, which was a much less systematic conviction that government was organized to protect the interests of the wealthy, and therefore all government was evil. True justice could come only when government was destroyed.

In the coal mines of Appalachia during the 1870s, as many mines were shut down because of the depression, a group called the Molly Maguires became notorious, even legendary, for their strong-arm tactics in dealing with mine operators. The Mollies were able to wring a few concessions from operators in 1876 by attacking replacement workers sent in to replace striking workers. The "scabs" hurried away and the owners had no choice but to reach a more generous settlement. But the success was short-lived. Twenty Mollies were arrested for murder. During their trials, several Pinkerton guards, who had gone undercover and infiltrated the Mollies, testified against them. Historians have determined that much of the Pinkertons' testimony and the other evidence used to convict these men was suspect. Nevertheless, all

The town of Pottsville, located in the coal region of northeastern Pennsylvania, was the site of the dramatic events and trial surrounding the conflict between the Molly Maguires and the Pinkertons in 1877. (Library of Congress)

twenty Mollies were convicted and executed in Pottsville, Pennsylvania, in 1877, primarily on evidence presented by the Pinkerton agents. This episode helped earn the Pinkertons the eternal enmity of organized labor.

The successful destruction of the Molly Maguires caused many unions to rethink their methodology. Most of those that represented skilled workers decided to purge their rolls of more politically minded and radical members, and to focus their efforts on representing a specific group of workers. The AAISW was formed in the wake of the Molly Maguire trials with the stated goal of looking out for the interests of skilled steel workers to keep them from being lumped together with more radical groups.

The AAISW also wanted to protect its members from being lumped in with unskilled workers, which would drag down wages and make it more difficult to negotiate with the owners. One of the threats to wages was the influx of immigrants into the United States. The steel and mining regions of Pennsylvania attracted large numbers of immigrants, particularly from Hungary and other eastern and southern European countries. There was inevitable tension between these new Americans and those who had been born in the United States.

The climactic event in the U.S. labor movement prior to Homestead occurred on May 4, 1886, at Haymarket Square in Chicago, Illinois. That spring, a strike had been called that was part of a larger movement through-out the industrial Northeast and Midwest. This general, or mass, strike was to fight for a universal eight-hour day. The demand for a three-shift, eight-hour working day, as opposed to the two-shift, twelve-hour day, had become a rallying cry for the entire labor movement. The cause even had the catchy "Eight-Hour Song":

> We want to feel the sunshine;
> we want to smell the flowers;
> We're sure that God has willed it,
> and we mean to have eight hours.
> We're summoning our forces
> from shipyard, shop and mill:

Eight hours for work, eight hours for rest,
eight hours for what we will.

The eight-hour workday had temporarily bonded together a movement that was usually fragmented by philosophical, religious, ethnic, and class divisions. Soon the tensions between skilled and unskilled, Catholic and Protestant, Socialist and non-Socialist, and white and black, would reemerge to divide the various labor and political organizations. But that May, when a general strike demanding the eight-hour day was called, the response was overwhelming.

In Chicago, where the labor movement was heavily influenced by socialists and anarchists, the strike quickly took on militant overtones. There was a great deal of local tension because of the ongoing conflict at the Cyrus McCormick Harvesting Machine Company, where a strike had been going on intermittently for years. McCormick was determined to rid his company of unions. When he had locked out union employees and persuaded the local police to provide protection for replacement workers, the strike had become violent.

Two workers were killed in a clash with police in Chicago on May 3. The next day, two local labor leaders were scheduled to speak against police brutality at Haymarket Square. About 3,000 workers had gathered by midafternoon when the speakers began. As the day turned to night, the crowd was still present, listening to speakers, or simply milling around and talking. Then, at

The deadly Haymarket riot of May 1886, spurred by workers' demands for an eight-hour workday, is thought to have been the inspiration for making May 1st International Workers' Day in many countries around the world. (Library of Congress)

10:00 PM, the police suddenly arrived and began trying to break up the rally. At that point, someone threw a bomb that exploded and killed a policeman instantly. The enraged police then opened fire into the mostly unarmed crowd. Panic ensued and in the melee seven policemen were killed, mostly from shots fired by their fellow officers, and eight civilians died. Dozens of people were wounded.

Over the next days police arrested many more union leaders and organizers. Eventually, eight strike leaders were tried for inciting murder. All were convicted. One committed suicide in his cell, three were executed, and four served life sentences.

The Haymarket Square riot, or massacre, depending

on the point of view, became a public-relations nightmare for the labor movement. The mostly anti-union press, aided by the wealthy owners and their political supporters, were able to place the blame for the tragedy on the strikers. It was a turn of events that did not go unnoticed by Carnegie and Frick, or by the leaders of the AAISW.

Responding to the bad publicity, the AAISW was determined to keep radicals out of the union and to focus on protecting the interests of members. In 1887, it linked up with four other skilled labor unions to form the

AFL and labor movement leader Samuel Gompers. (Library of Congress)

American Federation of Labor (AFL), which was under the leadership of Samuel Gompers. AFL's goal was to fight for higher wages and shorter working days. Gompers made it clear the AFL did not advocate socialism or general social or political change. He hoped to usher in a new era of labor-management relations, in which the groups could sit down and negotiate with goodwill and reach accords that benefited both sides. The future would hold the answer to how well this new strategy worked.

5.
Buying Trouble

T he original owner of Homestead, the Pittsburgh Bessemer Steel Company, had been founded by a group of Pittsburgh businessmen who considered Carnegie to be an enemy. Carnegie's dominant characteristic was a double-sidedness that allowed him to praise labor in the abstract but attack it in the specific. He had the same relationship to many of the wealthier citizens of Pittsburgh. He was dependent on them for advancement and eagerly learned how to mimic their manners and customs. At the same time, he bore a deep-seated resentment of those who were born into wealth and advantage and made defeating them in business one of his central preoccupations in life. Along the way, he managed to antagonize a sizable segment of the Pittsburgh aristocracy as they discovered the young man they had adopted as a student was outdoing his teachers. The men who formed Pittsburgh Bessemer had as one of their stated goals to compete directly with Carnegie and to undercut his prices.

The steel manufacturing business was highly competitive. Carnegie was usually under intense price pressure. Over the years he would occasionally reach agreements with competitors not to undercut the price of the steel they sold. But these price-fixing arrangements, which are illegal today, inevitably collapsed. As the demand increased for steel to be used in railroad, construction, shipbuilding, and other enterprises, and new technologies made production easier, more people entered the business. Eventually, the cutthroat competition threatened the entire market, and the steel industry would consolidate into a few large companies. But during the 1880s and 1890s, Carnegie Steel consistently faced intense competition.

This pressure naturally forced Carnegie and other manufacturers to concentrate even more on costs— particularly labor costs. When Carnegie bought the steel works at Homestead, he knew the union was part of the package. The union's refusal to accept lower wages and longer hours, and Pittsburgh Bessemer's failure to drive them out, was one of the reasons he was able to snap it up at a bargain price. Frick was still relegated to running the coke operation when the purchase was finalized. However, it would soon be left up to him to find a way to succeed where Pittsburgh Bessemer had failed.

A view of the steel mill at Homestead. (Library of Congress)

There were other issues at Homestead, besides the union, that had to be taken care of first. After the purchase, Carnegie closed the mill and began refitting it to make structural steel instead of rails. It would take until 1885 for Homestead to return to full capacity. A few years later, Carnegie would buy a parcel of adjacent land and build a mill to make steel armor for the navy. This new division at Homestead would only be in operation a short period before the strike closed it down.

The conversion at Homestead also meant a large investment in new equipment, which made the plant more efficient. Although always conservative about spending money, Carnegie never hesitated to invest in new equipment that would save money in the long run. At Homestead, new open-hearth ovens were installed in order to use a less expensive steel-making process. Homestead also implemented a "direct rolling" system for after the steel was cooked; it eliminated steps from the cooling process.

These equipment modernizations had a negative impact on the AAISW because they decreased the need for labor, which meant fewer union members. Other changes turned what had been more highly-paid skilled jobs into lesser-paying unskilled work. It had been a similar transition toward mechanization that had driven Carnegie's father out of the weaving business.

One example of a job lost to innovation was puddling, which involved the tending of the process of heating the

A steel laborer puddling, where he works up his ball of molten pig iron in the open air until it loses its carbon and becomes wrought iron. (Library of Congress)

pig iron to a temperature high enough to remove the excess carbon. The puddling process was time-consuming and performed by highly skilled workers. Carnegie, in his constant effort to improve efficiency, had closed the puddling furnaces in his steel mills. The puddlers who lost their jobs had been mostly union members.

Carnegie had his first taste of labor trouble at Homestead in 1889, right before he reorganized his steel companies and made Frick president in charge of operations at all the plants. The man in charge of Homestead in 1889 was William Abbot, who had joined the company as a clerk and worked himself into a partnership.

Homestead's contract with the AAISW was due to expire in the summer of 1889. Carnegie was determined to reduce the wage scale at his new mill by 25 percent, which would be on par with the scale at his Edgar Thompson works. He and Abbot met and worked over the figures and how they would be presented to the union leadership. Carnegie was willing to recognize the union if they accepted the new salaries.

Before the negotiations with the AAISW were over, Carnegie left for his annual summer trip to Europe. While he was gone, the dam upriver in Johnstown, Pennsylvania, gave way, and hundreds of working people lost their lives downstream. When it was discovered that the dam collapse was due to shoddy workmanship, and that it had been constructed to clear land for an exclusive hunting club for Carnegie, Frick, and other wealthy Pittsburgh families, there was a bitter reaction from the

The flood at Johnstown was the first major disaster relief effort handled by the new American Red Cross, led by Clara Barton. It remains one of the greatest disasters in U.S. history. (Courtesy of the Granger Collection.)

workers and citizens who had suffered. The Homestead members of the AAISW were no exception.

When Abbot attempted to force through the changes demanded by Carnegie, the union went out on strike. Abbot wavered in his response. First, he tried to hire local strikebreakers but to no avail. His next step was to ask the local law enforcement to come to his assistance and protect the strikebreakers. But the workers drove away the sheriff and his deputies and retained control of the works. Finally, Abbot, much to Frick's disgust, threw in the towel and signed an agreement with the union. The union did agree to the new wage structure, but in return it forced Abbot to recognize it as the official representative of the skilled workers that made up its membership, and to allow the next contract to expire in three years, on July 1, 1892.

By the end of the 1889 strike, the AAISW could proudly claim that it had stood down the owners and managers of Homestead twice. First, in 1883, it broke the back of Pittsburgh Bessemer. Now it had won over the mighty Carnegie Steel. It seemed that the more moderate approach to unionization, as opposed to the political, radical method of earlier unions, was the best path. Things had got tense during the strike, particularly when the union had turned the deputies away from the mill, but overt violence had been avoided. Abbot had not called in the Pinkerton Agency, and both sides had, in the end, made compromises. Maybe Samuel Gompers was right and this more moderate approach was the key to settling labor and management disputes. It would only be three years before the newer tactics would be put to another test.

Talks Begin

When he became president of Carnegie Steel Company and was placed in charge of operations for all the mills, Henry Frick was determined that he would rid Homestead of the AAISW. His only fear was that when the confrontation came, Carnegie would betray him, as he had in the coke strike, and force him to sign an agreement with the union. As 1892 approached, Frick had to contend with AAISW's demands on one side and Carnegie on the other.

Carnegie, for his part, claimed to have learned his lesson from past dealings with Frick and seemed to know he had to let him manage as he thought best. Carnegie had also been deeply disappointed by Abbot's acquiescence to the union in 1889, to the extent that Abbot was eventually relieved of his duties as manager. It is doubtful Carnegie ever considered running the risk of losing the man who had already become his most gifted lieutenant. And while he might have held sentimental attachment to the workers, Carnegie's true passion was for containing costs. Frick could be reasonably sure that he would have Carnegie's support in 1892.

The first question for Frick was to decide if he even wanted to talk with union leaders. To talk with the union was to recognize its existence and its authority as the representative of the skilled workers. Frick probably would have preferred to ignore them. But Abbot had recognized the AAISW in the 1889 contract, which meant Frick could be charged with bad faith if he unilaterally decided to not recognize them. There was also the question of public relations, particularly if he hoped to get assistance from law enforcement and politicians in the case of a shutdown. He had no choice but to at least go through the motions of negotiating.

The talks between Frick and the union leaders began in February 1892. He was joined by John Potter, the superintendent at Homestead. The union was represented by Hugh O'Donnell, a heater in the mill; William Roberts of the armored plate division; and Hugh Ross, who worked in the cold cutting. O'Donnell emerged as the principal leader. He had worked for Carnegie for years and had been principally responsible for the 1889 agreement. He had also worked at Edgar Thompson and had seen several men die in the plant. Over the years he had grown bitter at the ruthless focus on efficiency and

AAISW representative Hugh O'Donnell.

blamed it for the death of several comrades. Although he was not a radical, he felt deeply that Frick's leadership at Carnegie Steel had initiated a brutal regime that was no longer worth his loyalty. The events of the next weeks would only harden his determination and would eventually cost him a great deal personally.

The union had certain weaknesses that would challenge it in the days ahead. Only about eight hundred of the nearly 4,000 Homestead steel mill workers were union members; semi-skilled and common day laborers were excluded from membership. There was tension between the nonunion men and the union men since the union workers were skilled laborers and therefore paid much better than others in the mill. Union workers at Homestead, because of their previously negotiated contract, also made more money than workers in any other Carnegie factory, union or not. For these reasons, union workers had more impetus to cooperate with management because they had more to lose in a strike.

O'Donnell and his leadership committee agreed not to demand higher wages. Essentially, they wanted to simply extend the 1889 contract with all of its provisions. Of course, this would guarantee that if the price of steel rose, so did the wages of both union and nonunion personnel. This welded together the skilled and unskilled workers in a common interest and served to keep even nonunion workers loyal to the union. Day laborers knew that if the union was broken by a strike or any other means, Carnegie would employ only nonunion workers. This was enough incentive to keep them loyal to the union, although as unskilled labor they were not allowed membership in the union. It would be necessary for them to go on strike along with union members if it came to that.

An informal group photograph of Homestead steel workers in the 1880s.
(Carnegie Library of Homestead)

Ethnic differences also weakened the AAISW. The Scottish, Irish, Welsh, American, and English members tended to focus on the needs of their fellow nationals rather than on the good of the union as a whole. They were brought together, however, in their contempt of the Hungarians and other new immigrants to the Pittsburgh area.

Carnegie and Frick were aware of the union's internal problems. They also knew that much of the public was aware of the union's reputation for protecting poor workers. In the mills where union members had the authority to hire and fire, most union leaders automatically favored strong union members and members of their own nationalities. This favoritism resulted in a certain amount of incompetence. One union official admitted, "We kept men employed who ought to have been fired, and that wasn't right. But what could we do. . . . There is no way of keeping such men out of the union and their votes count for just as much as those of the better sort."

As the 1892 talks began, O'Donnell did have what he thought was one advantage in a showdown. The Homestead works had a $4 million contract to produce armor plate for the United States Navy. He and other union leaders thought that Frick would not want to provoke a strike that would jeopardize these contracts. This turned out to be a miscalculation.

There were three main issues in the negotiations. First, the 1889 agreement had adopted a sliding scale wage pegged to the price of steel. Wages went up as prices increased, down if prices dropped. There was a floor below which wages could not drop, regardless of how low prices went, but no ceiling to limit wages if prices took a sudden spike. Frick wanted a wage ceiling as well as a wage floor. The union pointed out that in 1889 it had agreed to a wage-scale reduction and refused to accept another this time.

The second issue also concerned wages, which were based on the quantity of steel produced—the so-called tonnage rate. The more steel produced, the higher the rate of pay. Frick insisted that most of the production increases at Homestead were due to improvements in the plant and equipment and that it was unfair for the company to invest in modernizing and then be forced to pay higher wages that were the result of their investments. The union countered that the new machinery had already led to layoffs, which allowed the company to save wages because more steel was produced with fewer workers. Now, union leaders argued, the owners wanted to further benefit by lowering pay for the workers who remained.

The third issue concerned timing. The union had insisted that the 1889 contract expire in the middle of the summer, on July 1, 1892. There was more than one reason for this demand. First, summer was obviously a better time to strike than winter, if that became necessary. Second, the demand for steel, particularly for the construction steel made at Homestead, was higher in the summer. This put pressure on the company to settle. It was for these same reasons that Frick insisted any new agreement would expire on December 31. Frick had another justification for his position that he put out for public consumption. Ending the labor contract with the calendar year would allow the company to more accurately plan for the upcoming year, he said, in determining the numbers of workers based on projected sales.

Frick had a knack for offering arguments that sounded reasonable on the surface but hid his true motives. His main goal was to give the appearance of negotiating in good faith with the union while ensuring no real progress could be made. Frick was successful in that the only concrete decision made was to establish June 24 as the

Henry Clay Frick in his middle age. (Library of Congress)

deadline for a new agreement. After that date, Frick warned, he would not negotiate with the union and would be free to deal with each worker on an individual basis.

It is doubtful that Frick was ever negotiating in good faith. Talks began in February, and before he sailed for England in April, Carnegie sent a notice to Frick that he said he wanted posted and published. The missive stated that because the majority of Carnegie employees were nonunion, the minority who were in the union would have to leave it. It would not work, Carnegie said, for a minority to be represented by a union and the majority left to shift for themselves. Carnegie claimed it was his concern for fairness that prompted him to do away with the union.

Frick, who had no illusions that such a transparent appeal would sway the workers to leave the union, realized that the notice, if posted, would only serve to reveal management's true intentions and toughen the resistance. He convinced Carnegie there was nothing to be gained from posting it.

Although Frick was far too savvy to admit it, he was probably delighted to see the wobbly Carnegie leave for Europe that spring. Carnegie certainly seemed relieved to leave the upcoming showdown behind for Frick to deal with. "Of course you will win," Carnegie wrote from England, "and win easier than you suppose." There is no written proof that Carnegie knew exactly what Frick's plans were for dealing with the strike. What is known is that afterward, when the company was awash in bad publicity because of the tragic events, there would be a terrible falling out between the two partners. Henry Frick and Andrew Carnegie would go to their graves as bitter enemies.

After Carnegie left, Frick was free to make decisions. From the union's point of view, leaving Frick in charge was itself an act of provocation. Frick had a well-earned reputation for union busting. He was even said to have tossed a striker at his coke plant into the river during a short-lived strike in 1877. He might have been too old to throw a workingman into the river by 1892, but his determination remained steadfast.

During the first week of June, as it was becoming apparent to everyone that negotiations would not work and there was going to be a strike, the AAISW held its annual meeting in Pittsburgh. Among the speakers was John McLuckie, mayor of Homestead, mill employee, and union member. Hugh O'Donnell, the local union leader, also spoke. It became clear from these and other speeches that the entire AAISW considered the upcoming Homestead showdown to be a matter of life and death for their organization.

Another potentially explosive issue emerged at the convention, one that could work to the favor of AAISW. Benjamin Harrison had defeated the incumbent Democratic president Grover Cleveland in 1888, primarily on a promise to keep high tariffs (taxes) on goods imported into the United States. American manufacturers, such as Carnegie, supported tariffs because they allowed them to undersell foreign competitors. Tariffs also artificially inflated the price of foreign goods, which made them less popular among workers. However, Harrison and the Republicans had been able to convince some workers, particularly skilled workers such as those in the AAISW, that high tariffs protected their jobs and wages. Enough union members had deserted the Democrats, who were generally more supportive of their cause, for Harrison to squeak out a victory.

The same two candidates were locked in another tight race in the election year of 1892. During the AAISW convention, several speakers suggested they had been

Labor organizer and Homestead mayor John McLuckie.

duped into voting for Harrison. As one put it, "You men who voted the Republican ticket voted for high tariffs and you got high taxes." The union leaders made it clear the Republicans could not count on their votes in the upcoming election if Carnegie was allowed to crush their union.

On June 23, the day before Frick's deadline, union workers asked for more talks, and Frick agreed to meet. Once at the table, the union agreed to accept a wage floor set at a minimum of twenty-four dollars a ton, two dollars away from the twenty-two dollars per ton the management asked. Frick countered by offering to accept a floor of twenty-three dollars per ton. He also refused to even discuss anything but a December 31 expiration date for a new contract. Frick then reminded them that if there was not a settlement by the next day, he would no longer negotiate with the union. Union leaders turned to Homestead superintendent John Potter in hopes of making a deal, asking, "Do you think this is fair?" Potter responded that he could not help them.

In light of what was to come, it seems tragic that only a dollar separated the two sides on the most critical issue. It is likely, though, that if an agreement had been made on that point, there would have been conflict on another. Frick had probably accomplished what he wanted at the June 23 meeting. By offering to compromise on the wage scale but refusing to discuss other critical issues, he hoped to be able to portray the union as being unreasonable. He could then claim that his goodwill was rejected. This would be the last meeting between the two sides—time had run out. There were no more discussions.

On June 25, the day after the deadline, notices were posted in the mills saying that the company would communicate only with individual workers, not with union representatives. In this day, before any legislation protecting workers' rights to unionize, this was perfectly legal.

On that same day, Frick wrote a letter that would lead directly to some of the bloodiest violence in the history of the American labor movement. The letter was addressed to Robert Pinkerton, president of the notorious Pinkerton National Detective Agency. Frick asked

Allan Pinkerton established the Pinkerton National Detective Agency in the early 1850s and became famous in 1861 when he uncovered a plot to assassinate Abraham Lincoln. Pinkerton would later pass on the business to his sons Robert and William. The agency's logo of an eye with the motto "We Never Sleep" inspired the term "private eye." (Library of Congress)

Pinkerton to send at least three hundred guards to Homestead as quickly as possible. Frick later claimed that he hired the Pinkerton guards to protect the mill from vandalism. However, it is nearly impossible to believe that he did not know how combustible an act it was to bring in the Pinkertons. The agency had been involved in a number of violent clashes and left a trail of unsolved murders while working for mine and railroad owners during earlier strikes. Ever since their undercover role infiltrating the Molly Maguires and testifying at their trials, the Pinkertons had become the symbol of armed resistance to the union movement. Nothing Frick could have done would have been more certain to lead to violence.

7.
Forces
Assemble

Though negotiations were not officially ended until June 24, Henry Frick began making physical changes to the Homestead works in May. Clearly anticipating trouble to come, he ordered the construction of a fence around the mill. The fence was tall, over twelve feet high, and topped with strands of barbed wire. It was almost three miles long and completely surrounded the steel works. Platforms were built in intervals along the top and searchlights installed in observation towers so armed guards could maintain vigilant protection of the six-hundred-acre mill.

Previously, the town of Homestead ran right up to the mill. Now an ominous fence separated the two. The symbolism of what was quickly dubbed "Fort Frick" was obvious. Although the workers had dedicated half of each of their days to the mill for years and it was the source of their livelihood, it belonged to Andrew Carnegie, Henry Frick, and a few other stockholders. The erection of the fence was a bitter blow to the workers and served to increase tensions even more.

As it became obvious a strike was approaching, Hugh O'Donnell created a leadership team, the Advisory Strike Committee, which included five delegates from each of the eight Amalgamated Association union lodges represented at the mills in Homestead. Anticipating trouble from management, he organized both workers and townspeople into three military-like divisions and assigned schedules and duties for guards who would be posted at all possible entrances to the town. O'Donnell wanted to find a way to avoid bloodshed, but he also wanted to keep Frick from replacing union workers with strikebreakers. All the while, O'Donnell continued to insist that the issues of wages could be settled peacefully through further negotiations.

There was one obvious problem the AAISW faced as the strike deadline loomed—gaining the support of the nonunion workers. Although union leaders could argue that all workers benefited from their work, it was not guaranteed they would get the support of the nonmembers.

The building of the fence around the mill helped the union's cause. It convinced the workers there would be no easy resolution. The union was further strengthened when, on June 28, Frick closed the armor plate and open-

Mill workers walk along the street that bordered the "Fort Frick" wall.
(Carnegie Library of Pittsburgh)

hearth divisions, where some eight hundred men worked. O'Donnell seized the opportunity and had the Advisory Committee draw up a resolution saying that all employees at Homestead would join the AAISW and go on strike in support of the men just put out of work. He presented the proposal to Homestead workers on July 1, recounting the collapse of the negotiations, placing the blame squarely on Frick's shoulders, and asking for a vote of support. The resolution was approved by a large majority.

The vote of support for the union from the unskilled workers was a blow to Frick, who had hoped to drive a wedge between the union workers and nonunion workers. He responded by closing down the entire mill. By the end of July 2, the once mighty Homestead Steel works was quiet. Frick also released a statement declaring that when the mill reopened it would be operated nonunion.

Closing the plant was devastating to the entire town. Those who did not work in the mills relied on the salaries of those who did. Without mill workers, businesses in town would be without customers. And yet after Frick shuttered the mill, it became the goal of the workers to keep it closed. For the strike to succeed, they had to stop Frick from bringing in replacement workers. It was also essential that none of the present workers return to their jobs or the union would quickly crumble.

After July 2, Frick and the workers were set on a path that, in retrospect, seemed destined to end in conflict. The details of the dispute were not insurmountable in themselves, but it was clear to most of the participants that the details were not the ultimate issue. There was a larger question. Did the workers have a right to organize and to allow that organization, the union, to represent them in settling on wages and other questions concerning their working conditions? Or, as Frick insisted, was the mill private property in which each individual worker was hired at the discretion of the mill's owners and managers? This was the central issue in 1892 and remains the central issue in labor-management relations today.

On the evening of July 4, Frick sent a request to county sheriff William McCleary's office in Pittsburgh for deputies to protect the mill from vandalism he said had been threatened by the striking workers, although he offered no evidence of any such threats. Frick insisted the mill, which he referred to as "our property," was under threat from "a mob." He demanded that the sheriff do his duty to uphold law and order and send deputies to protect it.

McCleary, an elected official, was hesitant to anger so many voters, but had no choice but to respond to such a request from one of the wealthiest men in the state. McCleary and two deputies arrived in Homestead from Pittsburgh early on the morning of July 5 hoping to arrange to send deputies in later that day. He was welcomed by the Advisory Committee and shown around the mills. McCleary then announced that he was there at Frick's request to provide protection for the mill. He said he hoped the union would understand and would allow his men to do their duty.

O'Donnell held a quick meeting with the Advisory Committee—approximately fifty men. He returned to McCleary and made a stunning offer. At least one hundred, and as many as five hundred, of the strikers had agreed to be deputized to provide protection for the mill. Furthermore, they agreed to post a bond to assure that they would not engage in any vandalism or other destruction.

This was a shrewd move on the union's part. It made clear their intention to have a peaceful strike and not to engage in the type of activity Frick was accusing them of planning. But McCleary could not report to Frick that he had deputized the very workers Frick was claiming wanted to vandalize his property. He had no choice but to turn down the offer.

The Advisory Committee then held another brief meeting and returned to Sheriff McCleary with another surprise. O'Donnell announced that as of that moment the Advisory Committee was dissolved. As a body they were no longer responsible for what happened during the strike. They had wanted to show their goodwill by offering to protect the mill. But now it was clear Frick was determined to bring in armed guards and replacement workers. The Advisory Committee disbanded because they would not be responsible, as a group or as individuals, for what would happen when the strikebreakers arrived.

"Our responsibility ceases from this very moment . . . we are not responsible for what may hereafter develop," O'Donnell said. McCleary bowed and said, "I shall send my deputies this afternoon."

At six that evening, Deputy Cluely and the nine other officers were turned away by 2,000 armed, angry workers.

Although it is not known if Deputy Cluely or Sheriff McCleary knew the Pinkertons were on the way when they made their visits, Cluely was not making an idle threat when he warned the strikers that more armed men would soon be arriving at Homestead. He did not have to possess specific information to know that Frick was

Strikers linger outside the train depot at Homestead. (Carnegie Library of Pittsburgh)

determined to seize control of the mill and to assert his authority over the workers. Later, Carnegie would criticize Frick for his hasty actions. Carnegie's favorite method for dealing with a strike was to wait out the workers. But Frick was a different man. He wanted not only to break the strike but to send the message he would never tolerate such action in the future.

On July 5, the same night the armed workers turned away Deputy Cluely, at around 11:00 PM, three hundred Pinkerton guards arrived at Bellevue station, just west of Pittsburgh, about ten miles from Homestead. Upon their arrival the Pinkerton's commander, Captain Heinde, asked Sheriff McCleary to deputize his men. McCleary refused but did have a man escort the Pinkertons from the train station to the docks, where they were to board two barges, the *Iron Mountain* and the *Monongahela,* for the river journey to the Homestead Steel Works company dock.

The Pinkerton force was mostly made up of drifters, part-time workers, and even criminals on the run from police. An encounter between the undisciplined Pinkertons and the angry, rowdy strikers was almost

The city of Pittsburgh, located where the Allegheny and Monongahela rivers meet to form the Ohio, was ideally positioned for river travel. The Pinkerton forces took advantage of this accessibility to approach Homestead from the water.

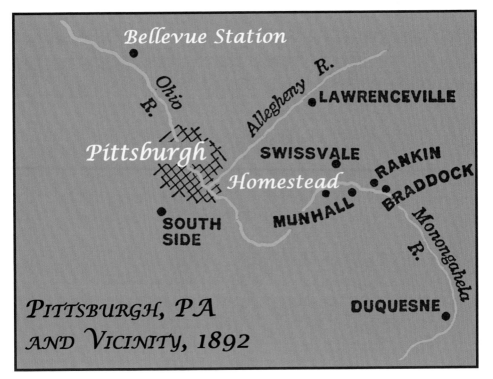

PITTSBURGH, PA
AND VICINITY, 1892

certain to result in violence, although John Potter, the superintendent of the Homestead Works, who accompanied the Pinkertons on one of the barges, gave orders to the hired strikebreakers to fire only in self-defense.

The Pinkertons were transported by barge down the river. The plan called for the Pinkertons to arrive in Homestead in the early morning hours, when the strikers would be asleep, land at the mill dock safely enclosed behind Frick's fence, and secure the mill before the workers could respond.

At around 2:00 AM on July 6, the two barges, towed by a tug boat called the *Little Bill,* headed down the river for the short journey to Homestead. The Pinkertons were armed with three hundred pistols and 250 rifles.

8.

The Battle of Homestead

What Frick and the Pinkertons did not count on as they planned their clandestine entry into Homestead, was the signaling system set up by the union. As soon as the barges left Bellevue, a telegram was sent to O'Donnell in Homestead warning that the Pinkertons were on the way. A small boat, the *Edna,* almost immediately left the Homestead dock, carrying armed men, to try to head off the barges. But Captain Heinde, following Potter's orders, ignored the *Edna* and refused to turn around. The *Edna* set off a whistle warning the townspeople that the Pinkertons were on their way.

It was nearing 4:00 AM as the barges approached Homestead, but the bank of the Monongahela River was lined with thousands of angry workers and their

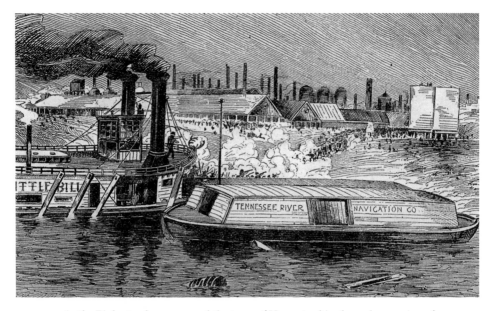

As the Pinkerton barges neared the town of Homestead in the early morning of July 6, they were met by throngs of angry citizens. (Library of Congress)

families. Most of the men were armed with rifles and handguns. The women carried knives and sticks. O'Donnell ran around, desperately trying to maintain order.

When the crowd realized the barges were heading for the company dock, they rushed the hated fence and quickly tore open gaps wide enough to stream through. They then stampeded onto the plant grounds. Although they were not able to stop the armored barges from docking, the armed crowd was determined the Pinkertons would not disembark from the boats.

As the crowd waited to see what would happen next, O'Donnell asked them to hold fire. There was a colorful collection of people on the dock that morning: men, women, and even some children. Elderly, white-haired

Margaret Finch busily rounded up supporters and encouraged the crowd to act. A steelworker's widow, Finch ran a popular saloon and was noted for her toughness. She had been one of the leaders of the dash through the fence to the riverbank. Brandishing a club, she was heard to remark, "Let me get at them. Let me get at them!" Finch at first thought the barges carried replacement workers, but was even more incensed when she realized it was full of Pinkerton guards. Following Finch's lead, the crowd began to shout, "Don't you land! Go back! Go back, or we'll not answer for your lives."

Also among the crowd was William Foy, a middle-aged English immigrant who was an unskilled laborer and not a union member. He was joined on the dock by Anthony Soulier, a skilled worker in an open-hearth department; Martin Murray, a skilled heater and union leader; and Joseph Sotak, who led a group of eastern European workers.

In the early morning light, Hugh O'Donnell stood on the riverbank and shouted to the men in the barges. "On behalf of five thousand men, I beg of you to leave here at once . . . if you remain there will be more bloodshed. . . . In the name of God and humanity, don't attempt to land! Don't attempt to enter these works by force!"

Captain Heinde, speaking from the deck of the *Iron Mountain,* identified himself and the men as Pinkerton agents: "We were sent here to take possession of this property. We don't wish to shed blood, but we are determined to go up there [to the mills] and shall do so."

Heinde's orders were to lead three hundred Pinkerton guards to the Homestead docks and to remove any workers who did not comply with their request to leave the premises. These were his orders and he intended to carry them out. He was impatient with O'Donnell's request to show restraint and was personally loyal to the idea that unions were illegal and that owners could do what they wished with their property. He was, on the surface at least, a perfect man to carry out Frick's plans.

For a moment, neither O'Donnell nor Heinde spoke. Then O'Donnell, flanked by five steelworkers, shouted across the water, "Before you enter those mills, you will trample over the dead bodies of three thousand honest workingmen."

Heinde and the other agents who had joined him on the gangplank surveyed the scene. Hundreds of armed men and women filled the steep embankment overlooking the landing site and hundreds more could be seen heading toward the bank. Scores more townspeople had taken up positions on the railroad tracks upstream from the company wharf and others had gathered on the opposite shore of the Monongahela River.

The quiet interlude was short lived. As the sky was beginning to grow light, Heinde ordered that the gangplank of the *Iron Mountain* be lowered. At this point, William Foy stepped to the foot of the plank. Five others followed him. Heinde told them, "There are three hundred men behind me, and you cannot stop us."

Foy shouted back, "Come on, and you'll come over

This photograph, taken sometime on the morning of July 6, shows the conflict between the workers and the barges taking place across the river. The scouting boat, Edna, *which had alerted the workers of the Pinkertons' impending arrival, can be seen in the foreground.* (Library of Congress)

my carcass." He then lay face down on the gangplank and waited, arm outstretched, revolver cocked. An angry Heinde slashed at Foy's head with his billy club, but in the process he tripped over an oar lying on the gangplank. One end of the oar flew into the air and hit a nearby striker in the face and knocked him down.

At this point two things happened almost simultaneously. Another worker rushed Heinde with a huge club, and two shots rang out in quick succession. One of the shots hit Foy, the other Heinde. There is still an unresolved dispute about whether a Pinkerton or a Homesteader fired first. On the barge, Pinkerton captain J. W. Cooper took the shots as a signal to open fire. He shouted a command, and a score of Winchester rifles fired into the crowd. The workers fired back. The firing went on for about ten minutes. One worker was killed on the spot, another died later of wounds, and two others were injured. As Homesteaders dashed to their aid, at least nine more were wounded. Reports are unclear but it seems that Pinkertons suffered about the same number of casualties.

When the firing stopped there was general confusion on both sides. O'Donnell was deeply upset. He had hoped to carry off the strike without violence. But, as the workers gathered behind the makeshift ramparts they had built from scrap iron lying around the yard, it was clear that the only thing that would stop the violence was if the Pinkertons left. If they stayed, it was sure to continue.

On the barges the Pinkertons and Superintendent Potter argued over their next move. Most of the men wanted to leave. Staying put where the men on shore could pick them off with sniper fire seemed to be a bad choice. But that was exactly what Potter insisted they do—hunker down until Sheriff McCleary arrived with deputies and the force of the law. He ordered that gun sights be cut into the barges so they could better fire on the townspeople.

Some of the Homesteaders had planned for this kind

of confrontation. They had gathered weapons and ammunition in union headquarters on the third floor of the Bost Building. Hearing rumors that thousands more sympathetic workers were coming from Pittsburgh and other cities to support them, they began to comb the town for more weapons. A hardware store owner gave out ammunition, and arms were distributed to anyone willing to fight.

O'Donnell was able to convince most of the women to move up the riverbank, farther from the barges. He enlisted the support of others to help him move the wounded to places where they could get medical care and helped the men build a long fortification above the riverbank from piles of steel beams.

Even during the lull the air was punctuated with occasional shots. Then, at around eight o'clock, the Pinkertons again attempted to unload off the barges. As the doors began to open the townspeople opened fire and the second stage of the battle erupted.

The townspeople had dragged a Civil War-vintage cannon across the river to the opposite bank. It was thought this would be a better position from which to fire at the barges. They loaded the cannon with steel scrap. The first shot tore a hole in the roof of one of the barges. Tragically, the next shot went horribly awry and struck a worker who had been standing in the mill yard. His head was blown off by the load.

Four strikers were killed in a matter of minutes. Those remaining had no way of knowing how effective their return fire had been. The deaths of their comrades enraged them. Any Pinkerton who showed his head through one of the improvised turrets was an immediate target.

As the summer sun rose and the day grew hot, the heat in the barges was almost unbearable. The trapped men, who were later described as cowards by Potter and their Pinkerton superiors, wanted to leave. They thought they were coming to guard a steel mill, not die trapped on barges. Many refused to fire and huddled on the floor, begging to leave.

Fires burn aboard the barges during the battle of Homestead. (Courtesy of the Granger Collection.)

Finally, Potter agreed to let the tug *Little Bill* return and pull the barges downstream, out of harm's way. But when the tug approached the dock, flying the Stars and Stripes because the captain was convinced the workers would not fire on the U.S. flag, the firing from the banks intensified. From the townspeople's perspective, things had advanced too far to allow the Pinkertons to leave. Their comrades had been killed and they wanted revenge. The captain of the tug threw himself on the deck and let the *Little Bill* drift out of range. Rescuing the trapped barges was out of the question.

By midday, five Pinkertons had been mortally wounded, and the workers were determined to drive out the rest of the agents. First, they filled a raft with barrels of oil, lighted it, and sent it drifting toward the barges— but it burned out before reaching its target. Next, the strikers loaded a railroad freight car with oil and timber, set it afire, and attempted to roll it down a track toward the barges. The car jumped the track. Then some workers found dynamite sticks, lit them, and threw them at the barges, but they all missed the mark, as did the rockets and Roman candles left over from the Fourth of July picnic. Firemen even tried pumping oil into the water and setting it afire, but the fire went out before it did any damage. As the afternoon shadows lengthened, it was becoming obvious that the conflict was at a stalemate. The Pinkertons were confined to the barges, and the strikers were running out of ways to get them off.

At three o'clock, William Weihe, president of the

AAISW, arrived in town with other union leaders. Weihe was a much admired forty-seven-year-old leader who had served a term in the Pennsylvania state legislature as a Republican. He was by nature a conservative man who tried to avoid strikes. He had been successful in restraining belligerent workers in earlier conflicts.

Weihe spoke with Sheriff McCleary and convinced him to send an emissary to talk with Frick. The emissary told Frick that he might be able to avoid further bloodshed if he agreed to negotiate with the workers. Frick refused and sent the secretary of Carnegie Steel to deliver a message to the workers: "Our works are now in the hands of the sheriff. . . . If it is necessary in his judgment to call out troops, he is the proper authority to do so."

Frick was holding tough to his position. The Pinkertons were there to protect his property and had been fired upon by a mob. It was a matter for law enforcement, not Carnegie management, to end. He put the responsibility for whatever happened next on the civil authorities.

McCleary had already sent an official request for state assistance to Governor Robert Pattison, saying that only his prompt intervention would prevent further bloodshed. The governor responded, "Local authorities must exhaust every means at their command for the preservation of peace." Even when McCleary sent him another plea, Governor Pattison insisted that the local authorities had not exhausted every means at their disposal to quell the disturbance. Pattison was dealing with the same political problem as McCleary. Both were elected officials trapped between antagonizing a large number of voters, who would be sympathetic to the strikers, and some of the most powerful men in the state. Pattison would prefer that this political crisis stay in McCleary's hands, at least until events gave him more political cover.

Meanwhile, O'Donnell convened a meeting of strikers and sympathizers in a mill building. He and Weihe both asked the townspeople to let the Pinkertons leave peacefully. But the time for reason had passed. The strikers replied "Kill them!" and "Burn them!" The two leaders were able to calm the townspeople and to hold off another attack on the barges, at least for the time being, by reminding the strikers that they would surely pay dearly for any assault.

By 4:00 PM, twelve hours after the barges had arrived, thousands of Homesteaders and people from surrounding towns had crowded the riverbank and the streets of Homestead, walking and talking and yelling threats toward the trapped barges.

When a contingent of three hundred steelworkers from a nearby plant arrived to help the strikers, the cheering was deafening. O'Donnell grabbed an American flag, climbed on a pile of steel beams, and asked the crowd to listen. Again, he asked them to let the Pinkertons leave quietly, and again the crowd noisily rejected the idea. They would settle for nothing short of surrender and demanded that the sheriff arrest all of the Pinkertons

This colorized image, originally published on the cover of the July 16, 1892 issue of Harper's Weekly, *depicts the Pinkerton guards walking the gauntlet after their surrender.* (Courtesy of the Granger Collection.)

for murder. O'Donnell then left to go to the barges where he hoped to negotiate a peace.

The Pinkertons had been meeting at the same time and had agreed to surrender. But doing so meant they had to trust the thousands of armed and angry people crowding the riverbanks not to kill or seriously injure them. Nobody wanted to be the first one to walk out on the deck and face the crowds.

But if they were going to get off the barges, they had no choice. Finally, two agents volunteered to step out first. At 5:00 they raised a white flag on the *Iron Mountain* and walked out onto the deck with their hands up. The crowd cheered. O'Donnell guaranteed them safe passage off the barge. Slowly each man climbed out of the barge and onto the deck where he was checked for weapons and then escorted up the riverbank.

As the men began leaving the barge, the still-enraged crowd pressed toward them and then formed two lines stretching from the barges up the hill. The tired, hungry, and frightened Pinkertons had to walk the gauntlet between these lines. As they stumbled up the hill, strikers and their sympathizers beat them mercilessly with sticks, umbrellas, anything they had in their hands. Some threw stones; others grabbed at their uniforms and tore them. Some of the agents were beaten so badly they lay on the ground, unable to move. All the while, the townspeople shouted and jeered and screamed insults.

In newspaper reports of the scene, journalists seemed most surprised by the viciousness of the Homestead

This illustration, also from Harper's Weekly, *shows angry Homestead rioters swarming outside the town opera house where the Pinkerton guards were temporarily imprisoned after their surrender from the barges.* (Courtesy of the North Wind Picture Archive.)

women. They described them as "fierce Amazons" and "shrews and harridans" and described their behavior as "warlike," "fiendish," and "frenzied." One report told of a woman who threw dust and stones into an agent's eyes. Another story told of a Pinkerton who was identified by someone in the crowd as a killer of a worker. He was beaten with a bull whip and when he lay on the ground, a woman rushed to him and beat him on the head with a large pole.

Another group that journalists later picked out as being particularly vicious were the immigrants, especially the Hungarians, who were sometimes referred to as "Huns." They reported seeing a Hungarian woman swing a stocking filled with iron at the agents' heads. One journalist summed up his opinion that the gauntlet was led for the most part by "unthinking Hungarians and foreigners."

These reports stereotyping and accusing these two groups—women and immigrants—would later serve to undermine the workers' cause. There was a great deal of antagonism toward immigrants in this era, and to paint the townspeople as enraged women and savage "Huns" was a public-relations victory for Frick and Carnegie.

Hugh O'Donnell and some other members of the disbanded Advisory Committee tried in vain to shield the Pinkertons from the blows. The guards finally managed to herd the Pinkertons through the town and into the Homestead opera house, where the frightened and hungry men huddled, protected by armed guards.

The Pinkertons remained in the opera house, some of them seriously injured, until 11:00 PM, when Sheriff McCleary arrived with officers of the AAISW. After a short conversation with Heinde and the other Pinkerton captains, the Pinkertons were quickly herded onto a train and sent back to Pittsburgh, where most were rushed away to New Jersey and a few to Chicago. Early the next morning, a search was done to make sure there were no Pinkertons hidden in the mill. None were found.

9.
Aftermath

The total number of deaths and wounds from the gun battle of July 6 is still unknown. The best estimates are that seven Pinkertons and nine strikers were killed, and over thirty wounded between the two groups. Some of the wounded workers might have avoided seeking treatment out of fear of being arrested or barred from working in Homestead again. An accurate count of agents wounded was not taken because of their quick retreat.

After the sun came up on July 7, the townspeople ransacked the barges and took anything they thought of value. Then they poured kerosene on the barges, set them on fire, and let them drift away. Homesteaders cheered as they watched the trail of smoke rise and then cheered more as the barges slowly sank into the river.

They did not know that, after learning of the battle, Carnegie had sent a telegram to Frick: "Never employ one of these rioters. Let grass grow over works."

In the next two days, funerals were held for the workers who had died in the confrontation. John E. Morris, the first Homesteader to fall, was a twenty-eight-year-old immigrant from Wales. He had been hiding on the roof of the pump house that overlooked the wharf. When the shooting stopped for a few moments, he raised his head to see what was going on, and a shot pierced his forehead, sending his body tumbling into a ditch sixty feet below.

Silas Wain, a twenty-three-year-old laborer and recent immigrant from England, had been standing in the mill yard when the old cannon, fired by the workers from across the river, exploded. A piece of iron went flying into his head, killing him immediately.

Nineteen-year-old Henry Striegel wounded himself with his gun as he prepared to fire. A Pinkerton agent then shot him in the neck, killing him instantly. Twenty-eight-year-old Peter Fares was on his way to a union meeting when he was mortally wounded. Thirty-year-old Joseph Sotak died from loss of blood from a gunshot wound, and George Rutter, a Civil War veteran, was carried from the field with a wound that ended his life eleven days later. In a eulogy at the First Methodist Episcopal Church, Reverend John McIlyar warned that "a suppressed volcano exists among American workmen, and some day there will be an uprising that will become history."

Except for Rutter, a native-born American, the men killed were immigrants, part of a wave that had come to America in the last decade of the nineteenth century searching for better economic opportunity. The men who died at Homestead were a cross section of the principal ethnic groups in Homestead—German, Welsh, British, Slovak, and native-born Americans.

The funerals, the feeling that the people of Homestead had triumphed, however temporarily, over the Pinkertons, and a basic belief in the justice of their cause gave new spirit to the workers. When a group of anarchists showed up advising them to seize the mills, the workers threw them out.

Anarchists are people who are opposed to all forms of government. They believe that individuals can reach their highest potential only if they are completely free from governmental restriction. Some anarchists believe that anarchy will come about through a natural evolution of society; others believe that organized action and terrorism are the only means to achieve their goal. Anarchists had hoped to find converts to their cause in the social and economic conflicts of the day. The unrest at Homestead had gained national attention, and the opportunistic anarchists hoped to turn the conflict into the beginning of a general revolt against the wealthy and the government. But the people of Homestead would not have their cause associated with the more radical politics of the anarchists.

The Pinkertons, too, had suffered death and injury in

the confrontation. The first Pinkerton to die was W. J. Kline, who was caught in the first volleys of shots exchanged around 4:00 AM. The second was Thomas J. Connors, a regular Pinkerton employee, who was struck in the arm by a bullet which severed his artery. Edward Speer, shot in the leg, died ten days later in a Pittsburgh hospital.

Although the townspeople and Homestead employees had cheered wildly when the Pinkertons were forced to flee, the more sensible among them, including O'Donnell, knew the company had no intention of giving up. From Scotland, Carnegie wrote, "We shall win, of course, but may have to shut down for months." Following orders from Frick to reassert company authority, Superintendent Potter attempted to enter the mill. But as he walked toward the mill buildings, he was stopped by a union guard who made him leave the town.

The next day Sheriff McCleary returned to Homestead. He said he would deputize any resident who wanted to be a policeman for the company. This time, no one took him up on the offer. He demanded that the strikers vacate the mill, but the workers refused. McCleary warned that this was not the end of the matter and took the train back to Pittsburgh.

McCleary, caught in a political bind, had some decisions to make, but he waffled, trying to find a smooth way out of the dilemma. He told the Pinkerton leader he would not deputize the Pinkertons right away but might consider doing so later. If they were deputized, the

Pennsylvania governor Robert E. Pattison ordered the state militia into Homestead.

agents would act with the full authority of the local law enforcement—something entirely too dangerous for McCleary to authorize.

Governor Pattison was McCleary's best hope. If the governor could be persuaded to send in the state militia, which could be used to quell riots and other disturbances that threatened life and property, it would solve the problem and move the political heat to Harrisburg, the state capital. But when McCleary asked the governor to call out the militia, Pattison was still wary of offending any supporters. McCleary telegraphed the governor again, insisting that the workers were an armed mob and that mere deputies could no longer control them. But Pattison still refused to call out the militia, saying again that "the civil authorities must in the end settle the differences."

That was Pattison's public statement, but at the same time he was secretly making plans to mobilize the militia. He had received too much pressure from Frick and his friends, all of whom had helped to make him governor, to delay any longer.

In Scotland, Carnegie initially refused to speak to the press. But he did issue a public statement: "I have implicit confidence in those who are managing the mills. Further than that, I have nothing to say."

Back in Homestead, the workers were cautiously optimistic. They placed sentries around the mill and grounds. They repaired the fence and distributed arms and ammunition to sentries.

On July 8, O'Donnell traveled to Harrisburg with a delegation determined to talk with Governor Pattison. They had heard rumors that the governor would mobilize the militia to take over the mills. O'Donnell assured the governor that the strikers were in charge of the mills and that all was peaceful. Pattison responded that he had received different reports, and that he was thinking about sending in troops. On July 10, Pattison ordered Major General George Snowden to arm 8,500 troops and take them to Homestead "to maintain the peace" and "to protect all persons in their rights."

John McLuckie, the mayor of Homestead and one of the strike leaders, told the press, "We will welcome [the militia]. We will accord to them the respect due to the

Located approximately two hundred miles east of Pittsburgh, Pennsylvania's capital city, Harrisburg, became the seat of decision-making regarding the government's response to the Homestead riot. (Library of Congress)

representatives of the grandeur and dignity of the great state of Pennsylvania." He and O'Donnell spoke to the 5,000 Homesteaders called together to hear the news that the militia would be occupying the mill. Fearful that any resistance on the part of the townspeople would result in more bloodshed, O'Donnell told them, "We can't fight the state of Pennsylvania, and even if we could, we cannot fight the United States government." McLuckie asked Homesteaders to welcome the militia with open arms because, he said, Pattison was a just man and surely would understand the plight of the workers once he saw that the townspeople were orderly and respectful.

McLuckie and O'Donnell organized the people into a procession to welcome the militia. They planned to meet Snowden at the railroad station and to assure him he was free to go anywhere he wished in the city.

Meanwhile, Snowden was preparing a surprise entrance into Homestead. He planned to arrive at nine on the morning of July 12. He and his troops disembarked at the Munhall station, near the steelworks, instead of at the Homestead station where the townspeople and strikers waited. The troops, seven regiments in all, quickly jumped off the train and proceeded down the tracks toward Homestead. When they arrived on Shanty Hill, they assembled their artillery pieces and trained their guns on the town below. Within twenty minutes, militia troops took the places of picketers who had been guarding the mill. Within half an hour, 4,000 troops had formed a line of battle facing the town. The Homesteaders looked across the river and saw sunlight glistening on metal rifles, bayonets, and other field pieces lined up on the hill overlooking them.

The Pennsylvania militia was known as one of the best in the country. They were efficient, highly trained, and equipped with new forty-five caliber Springfield rifles. Their officers were also efficient and adept at leadership and planning.

By ten o'clock, company officials, including Superintendent Potter, were in their offices in the mill. Snowden had set up an office in the school house. Disheartened at the rapid change in their fortunes, O'Donnell and McLuckie cancelled the parade and the welcoming committee.

A small delegation of Homesteaders did ask to speak

The state militia entered Homestead on July 12, 1892. (Library of Congress)

to Snowden. They told the general that they wanted him to know that both the union and the townspeople were fully ready to cooperate with them and help them in any way. "We come as representing the citizens of Homestead as well as the Amalgamated Association," O'Donnell told him.

"I am always glad to meet the citizens, the good citizens, of any country," said the general.

But the respectful tone did not last. When O'Donnell

said, "We have been peaceful and law-abiding citizens," Snowden cut him off.

"No, you have not," the general snapped.

For a moment O'Donnell was silent. Then he said, "General, we've got four brass bands, and we would like to have them and a parade of our friends pass in review before the camp."

"I don't want any brass band business while I'm here," said Snowden. "I want you to distinctly understand that I am master of this situation."

Taken aback, O'Donnell did not know how to answer. Snowden made it clear there was no need for him to reply. "I am here by order of the governor to cooperate with the sheriff in the maintenance of order and the protection of the Carnegie Steel Company in the possession of its property. I wish you good morning." Then he turned and walked away.

Snowden ordered his troops to stand sentry duty in the mill yards and on both sides of Frick's fence. He assigned some of his soldiers to use the *Little Bill* as a transport boat for supplies. The *Little Bill* now flew a state flag, signifying the authority of the government behind all its movements. Another tug brought replacement workers recruited from other cities. By the end of a week, about a hundred new workers were in the tugs waiting to land and take up employment.

Some of the children in Homestead actually enjoyed having the militia around. They watched as the soldiers in their snappy uniforms performed their formal drills

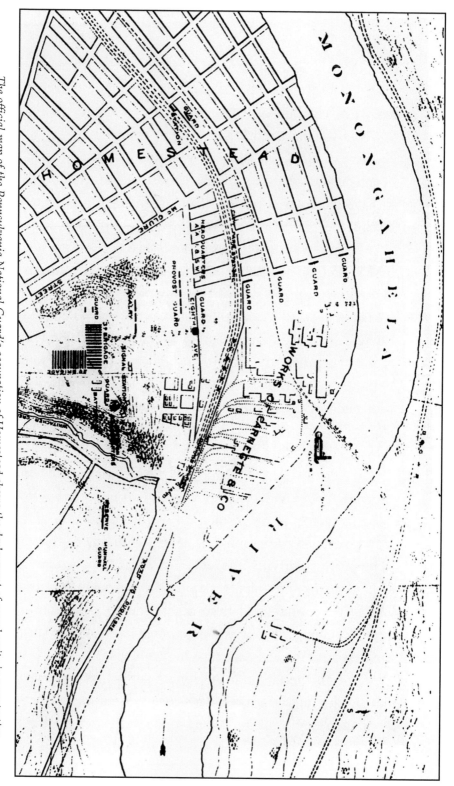

The official map of the Pennsylvania National Guard's occupation of Homestead shows the deployment of guard units in a protective semicircle around the steel works. (Annual Report of the Adjutant General of Pennsylvania, 1892)

with energy and precision. A few townspeople accepted jobs bringing supplies to the troops. By July 15, several of the furnaces in the mill had been lighted. Furious, the townspeople crowded near the mills to watch the smoke rise from the fires. Militia troops, who had orders to stay indefinitely, held them back with bayonets. Six former workers rushed forward and started to tear down the fence. They were quickly subdued by the militia.

The story of the battle of Homestead became a national sensation. This, combined with the fact that it was a hotly contested election year, led several congressmen to call for an investigation. One committee began holding hearings on July 12, 1892, less than a week after the battle. Both strikers and owners were called to testify. The strikers, who relished the opportunity to tell their side of the story, asserted that Frick had deliberately refused to negotiate in good faith because he wanted to drive the union out of Homestead.

In his testimony, Frick admitted that he had inquired about hiring Pinkertons to defend Carnegie's interests in the mills in Homestead early in June, before it was known that the AAISW would not accept the company's proposals. More evidence indicating that Frick's goal was to bust the union was that after the first ten days of the strike, there was no more talk of wages or working conditions in the mills. Further, Frick admitted that after June 24, when the union refused their terms, the company resolved to cease all negotiations with the AAISW and began to hire new workers.

The National Guard stands at attention along the "Fort Frick" wall in July 1892.
(Library of Congress)

However, two indisputable facts went a long way toward undercutting the union's cause and helped to tilt public opinion against it. The union had defied the request of the sheriff to let deputies guard mill property, and had treated the Pinkertons savagely after they had surrendered.

The committee also investigated the wage dispute that led to the strike and lockout. Frick testified that a reduction in the wage scale was necessary because the expensive new technology installed at Homestead decreased the cost of labor. He said that there was also a glut of steel on the market driving down prices. The workers, in their testimony, claimed that Frick and

Carnegie had purposefully flooded the market with steel billets to drive down prices as a negotiating tactic.

Frick claimed that distribution of wages was accomplished judicially between union and nonunion employees. O'Donnell and other union leaders pointed out that some workers received $12.20 a day and others $1.40 a day. Frick refused the committee's request for information about labor costs, claiming it was a business secret, but he said that the company had lost money on the plant for more than a year. In actuality, according to later studies of the profits at Homestead, mill profits went up by seventeen percent in 1891 and by sixteen percent in 1892.

As the investigation continued, union leaders tried to get their message to the public through the press. James Boyce, a leader in the AAISW, put out a statement. In part, it read:

> The people outside do not understand this Homestead position. Most of us, expecting continuous employment here, have put our savings into homes, which will be lost if we are to be driven away from this town. The Carnegie mills were built up by us, the great profits of the concern were made by us. Our labor was expended for Scotch castles and library advertising [a reference to the public libraries donated by Carnegie]. We do not say that Carnegie, Phipps and Company does not own the

mill property, but we do say that we have some rights in it ourselves.

Ultimately, the investigation bore no fruit. Frick was able to avoid answering questions about the real cost of labor by claiming it was confidential information that would hurt business if made public. The hearings came to a close with no laws changed and without any recourse offered to the strikers.

On July 16, workers found notices posted around the town stating that job applications would be accepted from former employees until six PM on July 21. The notices said that only workers who had not taken part in the disturbances would be considered for jobs. Anyone who did not apply by July 21 would be replaced. Most of the workers refused to apply, unable or unwilling to admit they had lost completely, and unwilling to be labeled scabs.

10.
Backlash

By the end of July 1892, Frick had nearly accomplished his goal of ending the AAISW as an effective union at Homestead. On July 19, work resumed in the open-hearth and the armor-plate mill, manned by strikebreakers brought in by train. On July 22, a large force of strikebreakers arrived on the tugboat *Tide,* and more came daily. Some were unemployed men eager for work; others had been employed elsewhere but came for the higher wages they could earn at Homestead.

Since the strike, there had been isolated incidences of violence between the former employees of Homestead and the replacement workers. The tension between those who had lost their jobs and those who had come to town to take them was understandable and palatable.

The union members seethed as the replacement workers flooded into their jobs, but it was the arrival of the African-American strikebreakers that infuriated them the most. This period was the beginning of the long backlash against African Americans that would last, in varying degrees of intensity, through the civil rights movement of the 1950s and 1960s. The attempt at Reconstruction over a decade before, following the Civil War, had failed and with it the last of the idealism that had followed that bloody struggle was dissipated. Hundreds of thousands of immigrants had come into the country since the 1860s. The economy had changed rapidly and there was much more competition for jobs. Economic insecurity was the prevailing concern in the industrial areas of the country.

During the 1890s, new, brutal racial segregation laws were passed across the South and other parts of the country. It was the decade of the infamous Supreme Court decision *Plessy v. Ferguson,* which established the principle of "separate but equal" in public facilities and schools across much of the nation. The townspeople of Homestead and the former employees of the mill were not free of racism, nor were most of the replacement workers who resented having to work along side African Americans. The violence was controlled by the militia, but hostility simmered.

The members of the former Advisory Committee, seeking a way to force Frick and Carnegie to deal with them, issued a public statement asserting the rights of the Homestead union members and those who went out on strike in support of them to continuous employment. It also insisted that the workers had the right to membership in any trade union or religious or ethnic group without interference by the company. The statement went on to declare that the union would pursue the members' interests in the courts and that it expected the state and national legislatures to guarantee the workers'

Replacement workers at Homestead line up to receive their pay after order had been restored and the mill was reopened. (Library of Congress)

rights. The union also pledged to refrain from violence. The statement was an attempt on the part of the union leaders to reassert its right to represent the workers and to make it clear the union considered it illegal not to hire a worker because he was or had been a member of the union. Frick ignored the union's statement and let it be known that he was still seeking workers to take the place of the strikers.

Although he had won the initial showdown with the union and was planning to continue his original plan to hire new workers and return the mill to full production as quickly as possible, Frick had several problems to contend with as a result of his policies.

One problem was political. Frick was a loyal supporter of the Republican Party, particularly its policy of high import tariffs that propped up the price of steel. He was under considerable pressure from national party leaders to be more accommodating toward the union. While most of them, including President Harrison, supported his right to lock out the union and to fire any employee he chose, there were many more workers than owners in America. While support for unions was not monolithic among the work force, they did enjoy wide and deep support in several key states, including Pennsylvania. But Frick refused to compromise his stand. Unlike Carnegie, Frick was not a man to show indecision in a crisis. He had determined the union had to go, and go it would, regardless of the political consequences.

More ominously for Frick on a personal level, Carnegie

began to send telegrams and letters from Scotland hinting that he disapproved of Frick's strong-arm tactics. In one telegram he called the events of July 6 a "fiasco" and wondered why Frick had allowed the townspeople to get between the barges and the mill. He hinted to other correspondents that his preferred method of dealing with labor troubles, to shut down the mill and wait for the strikers to run out of resources, would have been a better strategy. He lamented that Frick had taken aggressive actions, including hiring Pinkertons to try to seize the mill. This was the beginning of a rift between the two partners that would eventually lead to a bitter rivalry.

If Carnegie had sincere doubts about what Frick had done, he did not act on them when he had an opportunity to do so. On July 18, O'Donnell sent a letter to Carnegie asking him for his help in ending the strike. O'Donnell said the union would waive every right—except the right to have a union—and submit to any other regulation imposed by the company.

On July 28, Carnegie responded by sending a telegram to O'Donnell saying that the union proposal was not worthy of consideration. He also told Frick to use his own best judgment about reopening the mills. He and Frick both understood that O'Donnell's offer to compromise showed weakness on the part of the union and that this would be the perfect time to break the union once and for all.

The same day O'Donnell sent the letter to Carnegie, he learned that he was to be arrested for murder. Under pressure from Frick, McCleary had asked for and received arrest warrants for O'Donnell, Mayor McLuckie, and a few other union leaders. Each was charged with murdering a Pinkerton guard. O'Donnell and McLuckie were taken into custody a few days later. O'Donnell would be charged with another murder a few weeks later, and there would be more criminal charges to come.

Only two weeks after the conflict, Frick seemed to be in control of the situation. New workers were slowly restarting the furnaces; state and local officials were arresting union leaders. He had even negotiated some extra time to fill a large armor order. It seemed clear that his militant stance against the union had worked.

During these hectic days, Frick spent most of his time working in his office on Fifth Street in Pittsburgh. There he dictated letters and telegrams and met with countless visitors, working to get the plants up and running. One of the problems most in need of a solution was to find enough workers to return Homestead to full steam. Several of his visitors were from employment agencies seeking to capitalize on his need for skilled and unskilled laborers.

One of the men who called on Frick presented a freshly printed business card introducing Mr. Simon Bachman as the owner of an employment agency. Bachman made several attempts to see Frick and was finally told to come back on July 23, a Saturday, and perhaps Frick could see him then.

Simon Bachman's real name was Alexander Berkman,

Alexander Berkman in 1892.
(Library of Congress)

and he did not represent an employment agency. Berkman, a Russian-born immigrant to America, was actually an anarchist who had come to Pittsburgh to murder Henry C. Frick.

Berkman had come to Pittsburgh from Worcester, Massachusetts, where he ran a lunch counter and lived with Emma Goldman, another Russian immigrant. Both were active in the anarchist movement. The events at Homestead had angered Berkman and he decided to make a dramatic strike. If he killed Frick and avenged the deaths of the steelworkers, it would send a message to owners and workers alike that now was the time for the masses of people to rise up in revolt. In his mind, attacking Frick was attacking the whole capitalist system.

Frick was probably interested in meeting with Berkman when he returned that Saturday, at the appointed time, but he sent word through his secretary that he would have to reschedule. He was in a meeting with a company vice president. When the secretary told Berkman that Frick was busy, Berkman turned as though he was going to leave. But then he stopped and turned. Later, in his memoir, *Prison Memoirs of an Anarchist,* Berkman recounted what happened next:

> But quickly retracing my steps, I pass through the gate separating the clerks from the visitors, and, brushing the astounded attendant aside, I step into the office on the left, and find myself facing Frick.
>
> For an instant the sunlight, streaming through the windows, dazzles me. I saw two men at the further end of the long table.
>
> "Fr—" I begin. The look of terror on his face strikes me speechless. It is the dread of the conscious presence of death. "He understands," it flashes through my mind. With a quick motion I draw the revolver. As I raise the weapon, I see Frick clutch with both hands the arm of the chair, and attempt to rise. I aim at this head. "Perhaps he wears armor," I reflect. With a look of horror he quickly averts his

face, as I pull the trigger. There is a flash, and the high-ceilinged room reverberates as with the booming of cannon. I hear a sharp, piercing cry and see Frick on his knees, his head against the arm of the chair.

The first shot hit Frick in the ear and neck and penetrated to his back. A second shot hit Frick in the neck. Before Berkman could fire again, the company vice president jumped him and knocked the third shot wild. While Berkman and the vice president wrestled, Frick was able to pick himself up from the floor and grab

Berkman barges into Frick's office, pulls a gun, and shoots Frick. This engraved illustration of the attempted assassination was published in a contemporary periodical. (Courtesy of the Granger Collection.)

After his release from prison in 1906, Alexander Berkman went on to become a prominent leader in the U.S. anarchist, antiwar, and civil rights movements. In this 1908 photograph, Berkman (center stage) *speaks to a crowd in New York's Union Square.* (Library of Congress)

Berkman from behind. The three men rolled around the floor.

Berkman then pulled a dagger from his pocket and stabbed Frick in the hip, the right side, and the left leg. But the determined Frick refused to give up and threw himself on Berkman, pinning him to the floor. At that moment, other clerks rushed in and subdued the assailant. A deputy sheriff rushed in and aimed his gun at Berkman. Frick shouted, "Don't shoot. Leave him to the law but . . . let me see his face." Everyone looked at Berkman. He was chewing something. Immediately the sheriff suspected a ploy sometimes used by anarchists.

He forced open his mouth and found a capsule of fulminate of mercury. If Berkman had succeeded in biting open the capsule, they all would have been blown to bits.

When a doctor came to tend to his wounds, Frick refused chloroform while he was probed for the bullets. He wanted to stay awake to be better able to tell the doctor when he was getting near the bullets. After removing the bullets, the doctor sewed up and dressed the wounds. Amazingly, Frick returned to his work signing letters and dictating messages to his mother and Carnegie about the attempt on his life. He also sent out a press report saying in part, "I do not think I shall die, but whether I do or not, the Company will pursue the same policy, and it will win."

11.

"I'll See Him in Hell"

News of the attempted assassination flashed around the country. Although Berkman had no connection with the AAISW, his assassination attempt set off a backlash against the strikers and undermined their cause. The earlier violence had been reported in newspapers that were by and large sympathetic to Carnegie and Frick. Although they were subjected to some criticism for how they handled the strike, particularly Carnegie, who was pilloried for being out of the country, most of the major papers were instinctively on the side of capital. The stories had usually emphasized the "mob" nature of the events and suggested, or baldly claimed, that the strikers had fired the first shots and generally behaved poorly.

After the attack on Frick, even people who had been

sympathetic to the union began to turn against it. As soon as he began to recover from his wounds, Frick wasted no time in yoking Berkman together with the strike leaders who had already been arrested for murder. The story of his bravery in the face of attack, and his refusal to let the lawman shoot Berkman, also reflected well on Frick.

Another event made him a more sympathetic character. While he recuperated at his estate outside of Pittsburgh, Frick's infant son died, on August 3. The baby was less than a month old, having been born on July 6, the day of the battle at Homestead.

More than anyone else, the strike leaders knew that Berkman's blows had done more damage to them than to Frick. In summing up the impact, O'Donnell said, "It would seem that the bullet from Berkman's pistol, failing in its foul intent, went straight through the heart of the Homestead strike."

Frick returned to work soon after his son's death, and by the middle of August, 1, five-hundred men were at work in the mill. State troopers escorted the new hires to and from the mills as the former workers continued to picket outside. In town, support for the strike gradually began to slip. Some were disheartened and frightened as businesses faced hard times. The town council became torn between members who sympathized with the strikers and those who said they should end it and try to go back to work.

Frick continued to enlist politicians and law enforcement to exert pressure on the union. The state handed down more indictments of labor leaders on charges of murder and conspiracy.

By October 13, the situation had quieted enough for the last of the militia to leave Homestead. The union leaders were either in jail or in hiding, or forbidden by the terms of their parole to engage in union activities, and the remaining strikers were disheartened. By October 15, more than 2,000 men were working in the mill, including one hundred former workers. More new workers were being brought in every day.

A week later, Samuel Gompers, president of the American Federation of Labor, the umbrella organization that the AAISW was part of, came to Homestead. The failure of the strike struck a blow against his group, and weakened the belief that a union of skilled workers that avoided radical politics should be able to reach an accord with owners. He hoped to organize a boycott of Carnegie products, but despite a high-profile visit, Gompers was too late. Though the strike was not yet officially over, the spirit of Homestead had been broken. Carnegie had instituted a nationwide blacklist that kept strikers from being hired at other steel mills, and families were beginning to wonder how they would survive.

In the presidential election that November, a temporary victory was made for labor when Grover Cleveland returned to the political fray to defeat the incumbent, Harrison, largely because of widespread opposition to the high tariffs Harrison supported. But Cleveland's

The 1892 victory of Grover Cleveland and his vice president, Adlai Stevenson, is celebrated in the streets. Cleveland, thought to be a labor advocate, proved disappointing for his actions in ending the Pullman Strike of 1894. (Library of Congress)

return to the White House had little effect on the increasingly hungry and desperate Homestead workers.

At another meeting in Homestead, on November 17, 2,000 nonunion laborers and mechanics drafted a proposition that declared the strike over. There was nothing to be gained from trying to negotiate further with management. They asked that the union release them from their obligation to support the strike. The next day the union met and voted 224 to 129 to discontinue the strike. Less than twenty-four hours later, laborers and mechanics, all nonunion, applied for jobs. All were hired except those whose positions had already been filled by strikebreakers.

Frick and Carnegie congratulated each other in telegrams. Frick wrote, "Our victory is now complete . . . we
had to teach our employees a lesson and we have taught
them one they will never forget," to which Carnegie
answered, "Life worth living again. Congratulate all
around."

The aftermath of the strike continued. Some of the
strikers still had court cases facing them. There had been
132 indictments processed on charges ranging from
conspiracy, riot, and treason. Three murder charges went
to trial, including the one against Hugh O'Donnell. All
three men were tried and found not guilty, which was the
preferred outcome for Frick as well as for the men. The
last thing he wanted was to create martyrs to the union
cause. The rest of the indictments for the various charges
were also dropped.

There was also a larger case filed in the Supreme
Court of Pennsylvania charging the Homestead workers
with waging "war, insurrection, and rebellion against
the Commonwealth of Pennsylvania." The indictment
charged that the Homesteaders had committed treason
when they tried to control the mills by resisting the
Pinkertons. This line of reasoning suggested that resisting police officers was an act of war against the state.

As would be expected, the steel industry trade journals applauded this reasoning because it struck a blow
at unions. However, respected journals, such as the
American Law Review, stated that no reasonable person
could consider the activities of the Homesteaders as

treason. The labor press declared it an outrage that corporations should use civil authority as a weapon against employees. Ultimately, this case was also dropped.

Their defeat at Homestead ended the AAISW's effectiveness in the steel industry. It still had members among miners and among some iron manufacturers in the West, and was able to win concessions for its workers in places where it was difficult for owners to ship in replacement workers, but its once-powerful role in the steel business was over by 1900. Frick had shown the other steel manufacturers how to win the support of the local, state, and even federal government to help squash a strike. His argument that the mills were private property and that owners had the right to replace strikers with imported labor had won the day. This would continue to be the most effective strategy for corporations for over a generation, until laws were passed in Washington restricting their right to hire replacement workers.

The report of the Congressional investigation into the Homestead strike was eventually made public. It severely criticized the Homesteaders for their treatment of the Pinkertons, saying, "No brave man or good woman will maltreat a prisoner who is disarmed and has no chance to defend himself." But the legislators also chastised Carnegie Steel's management, saying that if Frick had tried to negotiate in good faith, "an agreement would have been reached between him and the workmen, and all the trouble which followed would thus have been avoided." The report might have raised the spirits of some union members and townspeople, but it did nothing to improve their lives.

Within the Homestead works, Frick and Carnegie now had total control over wages and working conditions. They wasted little time imposing a "cost saving" regime. A study done a few years later revealed how dramatic the wage changes were. For example, a roller who had earned $12.15 per ton in February 1892 averaged $6.00 per ton in February 1894. Over the same time frame heaters went from $9.55 to $5.25; tablemen from $6.94 to $3.20; and shearman from $9.85 to $4.09. Other studies found even sharper declines in wage scales at Homestead. These decreases became general throughout the industry.

Carnegie Steel also became much more proactive in keeping organizers out of its mills. One strategy for doing this was to hire Pinkerton agents as undercover workers. It was estimated that during the rest of the decade one out of ten Carnegie Steel employees was a secret Pinkerton agent. If a worker was suspected of having sympathies for the union, he was immediately fired. Others were fired for grumbling about working conditions.

The eight-hour day and overtime pay for working on Sundays was discontinued. Twelve-hour days were the standard, and men would be told on Saturday if they needed to show up the next day. Not to come in put one's job at risk. There was another severe depression in 1893, which meant for most of the decade there were plenty of unemployed workers and new immigrants, all eager to grab jobs from the fired workers.

The profits at Carnegie continued to grow, as did the amount of steel produced. Over the coming years, Carnegie was able to take advantage of the economic downturn as he had in the 1870s and continued to consolidate his hold on the Pittsburgh-area steel industry.

Although they had clearly won the struggle with the workers, the events at Homestead opened up a rift between Carnegie and Frick that continued to widen until it drove them apart forever. The rift was fueled primarily by comments Carnegie made to friends, Carnegie Steel board members, and a few reporters, suggesting that he did not approve of how Frick handled the strike. Carnegie let it be known that he would have simply waited the strikers out and would not have tried to force the issue by bringing in Pinkerton agents. When Frick learned of Carnegie's criticisms, he was angry but was able to keep his temper in check—for a while.

In 1896, Frick resigned as chairman of Carnegie Steel. After he retired from the daily running of the business, the tension between the two strong-willed men grew. There were fights over stock transactions and partnership agreements.

The final blow to their relationship came when both men decided it was time to try to sell the company and retire. Carnegie wanted to focus on giving money away to establish a legacy as a philanthropist. Frick had discovered a love for art collecting.

Frick found a buyer for Carnegie Steel, but when Andrew Carnegie discovered Frick had negotiated a broker's fee of five million—in addition to his own buyout—he angrily cancelled the sale. The two men held meetings during which tempers grew so heated that Frick threatened to throw Carnegie out a window. Frick soon resigned from the board of Carnegie Steel. He and Carnegie never met again.

Meanwhile, a group of investors put together by the great financier J. P. Morgan purchased Carnegie Steel for $480 million, the largest corporate buyout in U.S. history at the time. Frick pocketed over $60 million, Carnegie over $225 million, which made him the wealthi-

Through the mergers and acquisitions of his investment firm, J. P. Morgan & Co., J. P. Morgan had become the wealthiest man in America by the turn of the century. (Library of Congress)

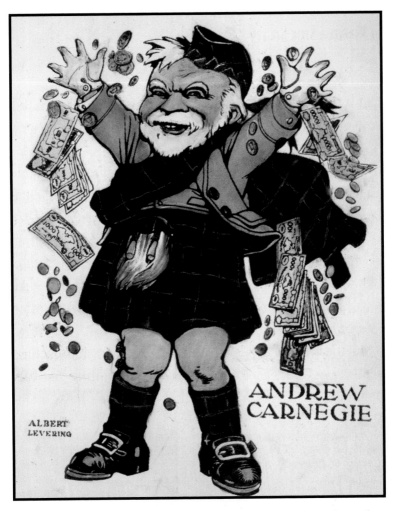

ALBERT LEVERING

ANDREW CARNEGIE

In his later years, Carnegie's transformation from steel magnate to benevolent philanthropist was often caricatured. (Courtesy of the Granger Collection.)

est man in the world. The new company, U.S. Steel Corporation, was immediately the largest company in the world.

In his later years, Carnegie continued to travel and to fund schools, universities, and, most famously, over 2,800 libraries, becoming the predominant benefactor of public libraries in the world. There are schools and concert halls in Pittsburgh and New York that bear his name. Frick continued to collect art and, at his death, his collection, displayed in his former house in New York, became the Frick Museum.

Frick never made an attempt to reach out to Carnegie after their final break. However, the more sentimental Carnegie did make one last effort. In the spring of 1919, as the eighty-three-year-old Carnegie neared death in his mansion in New York City, he called for a secretary. He handed the secretary a note and asked him to take it to Frick, who also lived in the area of New York often referred to as Millionaires' Row.

In the note, Carnegie acknowledged his approaching death. He told Frick he regretted their falling out and thought that it was beneath their dignity to have main-

Andrew Carnegie's beaux-arts style mansion on Millionaires' Row would later become home to the Smithsonian's Cooper-Hewitt National Design Museum. (Library of Congress)

tained the feud for so long. He asked Frick to come visit so they could make amends before death separated them.

At Frick's house, Carnegie's secretary was granted entry into the study and an audience with Frick. Frick, who had grown gray and thicker with age, read the note. Then he looked up at the secretary and said, "So Carnegie wants to meet me, does he?"

The secretary did not respond. There was a long pause as Frick stared menacingly at the secretary. Finally, he said, "Yes, you can tell Carnegie I'll meet him. Tell him I'll see him in Hell, where we both are going."

TIMELINE

1835 Andrew Carnegie born in Dunfermline, Scotland.

1848 Carnegie family immigrates to Pittsburgh, PA.

1849 Henry Clay Frick born in Westmoreland County, PA.

1855 Englishman Henry Bessemer invents a converter to manufacture inexpensive steel.

1856 Carnegie makes his first stock investment.

1872 Carnegie goes to England in the spring and sees the Bessemer conversion process; Carnegie founds his first steel company in November.

1876 Amalgamated Association of Iron and Steel Workers founded.

1882 Carnegie invests in H. C. Frick Coke Company.

1883 Carnegie acquires the Homestead Mill.

1886 Frick buys an interest in Carnegie's steel company; the massacre at Haymarket Square in Chicago kills seven policemen, four civilians, and wounds dozens.

1887 Frick becomes president of Carnegie Brothers and Company; American Federation of Labor founded.

1888 Benjamin Harrison defeats Grover Cleveland in the presidential election.

1889 The first strike at Homestead is resolved by a contract set to expire in 1892.

1896 Frick resigns as chairman of Carnegie Steel.

1919 Carnegie dies on August 11; Frick dies on December 2.

1892

February	Talks begin between labor and management; June 24 deadline is established.
April	Carnegie travels to England, leaving Frick in charge.
May	Frick builds a fence around the mill complex.
June 7	AAISW meeting in Pittsburgh authorizes strike if necessary to keep twenty-five dollars a ton as minimum payment.
June 19	Union agrees to accept twenty-four dollars a ton—Frick refuses the offer.
June 23	Management and union meet, no progress made.
June 25	Company announces it will speak only to individuals, not to union representatives.
June 28	Frick closes armor-plate and open-hearth divisions.
June 30	Contract expires.
July 1	Homestead workers vote overwhelmingly to support the strike.
July 2	All Homestead workers receive notices they have been fired.
July 5	Strikers twice turn away local law enforcement; Pinkertons arrive in Pittsburgh that night.
July 6	Pinkertons arrive at Homestead before dawn via barge; workers prevent them from disembarking and a gun battle begins; Pinkertons surrender around 5:00 PM.
July 10	Governor Pattison orders militia to Homestead.
July 12	Captain Snowden arrives in Homestead with 8,500 troops; Congressional investigation opened.
July 15	Mills restarted with nonunion workers.

July 18	Hugh O'Donnell offers to accept most of company demands; Frick refuses the offer.
July 23	Alexander Berkman tries to assassinate Frick.
October 13	Last of militia leaves Homestead.
November 8	Cleveland defeats Harrison in the presidential election.
November 19	Union votes to end strike.

SOURCES

CHAPTER ONE: American Dreams

p. 12, "Our instructions are to . . ." Les Standiford, *Meet You in Hell: Andrew Carnegie, Henry Clay Frick, and the Bitter Partnership that Transformed America* (New York: Crown Publishers, 2005), 154.

p. 13, "You fellows will . . ." Ibid.

p. 18, "The powerful jets of . . ." Ibid., 91.

p. 18, "created his own mold," Ibid.

p. 19, "When the blast is . . ." Ibid., 113-114.

p. 19, "Everywhere in the enormous . . ." Leon Wolff, *Lockout: The Story of the Homestead Strike of 1892* (New York: Harper & Row Publishers, 1965), 36.

p. 21-22, "as squalid as could . . ." Ibid., 30-31.

CHAPTER TWO: One Immigrant's Story

p. 23, "The right of the . . ." Peter Krass, *Carnegie* (Hoboken, NJ: John Wiley & Sons, 2002), 215.

p. 28-29, "It gave me the first . . ." Andrew Carnegie, *The Autobiography of Andrew Carnegie* (Boston: Northeastern University Press, 1920), 87.

p. 30, "Put all good eggs . . ." Ibid., 170.

CHAPTER SIX: Talks Begin

p. 64, "We kept men employed . . ." John Fitch, *The Steel Workers* (Pittsburgh: University of Pittsburgh Press, 1989), 102.

p. 67, "Of course you will . . ." Standiford, *Meet You in Hell,* 122.

p. 69, "You men who voted . . ." Ibid., 128.

p. 70, "Do you think . . ." William Serrin, *Homestead: The Glory and Tragedy of American Steel* (New York: Random House, 1992), 72.

CHAPTER SEVEN: Forces Assemble

p. 76, "our property . . . a mob," Standiford, *Meet You in Hell,* 150.

p. 77, "Our responsibility ceases . . ." Paul Krause, *The Battle for Homestead* (Pittsburgh: The University of Pittsburgh Press, 1992), 314.

CHAPTER EIGHT: The Battle of Homestead

p. 83, "Let me get at . . ." Krause, *The Battle for Homestead,* 17.

p. 83, "Don't you land! . . ." Ibid., 18.

p. 83, "On behalf of five . . ." Ibid.

p. 83, "We were sent here . . ." Ibid.

p. 84, "Before you enter . . ." Ibid.

p. 84, "There are three hundred . . ." Ibid.

p. 84-85, "Come on, and you'll . . ." Ibid., 19.

p. 90, "Our works are now . . ." Ibid., 25.

p. 90, "Local authorities must . . ." Ibid., 29.

p. 94, "fierce Amazons," Ibid., 322.

p. 94, "shrews and harridans," Ibid.

p. 94, "warlike," "fiendish," "frenzied," Ibid.

p. 95, "unthinking Hungarians . . ." Ibid., 323.

CHAPTER NINE: Aftermath

p. 97, "Never employ one . . ." Serrin, *Homestead,* 82.

p. 97, "a suppressed volcano . . ." Krause, *The Battle for Homestead,* 312.

p. 99, "We shall win, of . . ." Serrin, *Homestead,* 83.

p. 101, "the civil authorities . . ." Krause, *The Battle for Homestead,* 32.

p. 101, "I have implicit . . ." Serrin, *Homestead,* 83.

p. 101, "to maintain the peace . . . in their rights," Krause, *The Battle for Homestead,* 334.

p. 101-102, "We will welcome . . ." Ibid.

p. 102, "We can't fight . . ." Ibid.

p. 104-105, "We come as . . . master of this situation," Serrin, *Homestead,* 85.

p. 105-106, "I am here by order . . ." Krause, *The Battle for Homestead,* 338.

p. 109, "The people outside . . ." Ibid., 339.

CHAPTER TEN: Backlash

p. 115, "fiasco," Standiford, *Meet You in Hell,* 188.

p. 118-119, "But quickly retracing . . ." Ibid., 209.

p. 120, "Don't shoot. Leave . . ." Serrin, *Homestead,* 87.

p. 121, "I do not think . . ." Ibid., 88.

CHAPTER ELEVEN: "I'll See Him in Hell"

p. 123, "It would seem that . . ." Ibid., 88.

p. 126, "Our victory is . . ." Milton Meltzer, *Bread and Roses* (New York: Alfred A. Knopf, 1967), 144.

p. 126, "war, insurrection, and rebellion . . ." Krause, *The Battle for Homestead,* 349.

p. 127, "No brave man . . ." Fitch, *The Steel Workers,* 131.

p. 127-128, "an agreement would . . ." Ibid.

p. 133, "So Carnegie wants . . . are going," Standiford, *Meet You in Hell,* 15.

BIBLIOGRAPHY

Burgoyne, Arthur. *The Homestead Strike of 1892.* Pittsburgh: University of Pittsburgh Press, 1979.

Carnegie, Andrew. *The Autobiography of Andrew Carnegie.* Boston: Northeastern University Press, 1986.

Colman, Penny. *Strike! The Bitter Struggle of American Workers from Colonial Times to the Present.* Brookfield, CT: The Millbrook Press, 1995.

Fitch, John A. *The Steel Workers.* Pittsburgh: University of Pittsburgh Press, 1989.

Krass, Peter. *Carnegie.* Hoboken, NJ: John Wiley & Sons, 2002.

Krause, Paul. *The Battle for Homestead 1880-1892: Politics, Culture, and Steel.* Pittsburgh: University of Pittsburgh Press, 1992.

Meltzer, Milton. *Bread and Roses.* New York: Alfred A. Knopf, 1967.

———. *The Many Lives of Andrew Carnegie.* New York: Franklin Watts, 1997.

Muralo, Priscilla and A. B. Chitty. *From the Folks Who Brought You the Weekend.* New York: The New Press, 2001.

Serrin, William. *Homestead: The Glory and Tragedy of an American Steel Town.* New York: Random House, 1992.

Standiford, Les. *Meet You in Hell: Andrew Carnegie, Henry Clay Frick, and the Bitter Partnership that Transformed America.* New York: Crown Publishers, 2005.

Wolff, Leon. *Lockout: The Story of the Homestead Strike of 1892.* New York: Harper & Row Publishers, 1965.

WEB SITES

http://history.osu.edu/projects/HomesteadStrike1892/
An Ohio State University page that links to several primary-source documents reporting on the events of the strike.

http://www.carnegie.org/sub/kids/index.html
The Carnegie Corporation of New York, which continues the mission set forth by Andrew Carnegie when he founded it in 1911, has fact- and photo-filled pages specifically for younger audiences.

http://www.aflcio.org/
Labor unions continue to be an important part of the American economy. In 1955, the AFL merged with another union, the Congress of Industrial Organizations, to form the AFL-CIO, which is today nine million members strong.

http://www.frick.org/
The art Henry Frick acquired can still be seen today at the Frick Collection in New York City.

http://www.nlrb.gov/nlrb/home/default.asp
The National Labor Relations Board was created in 1935 and oversees the interaction between private corporations and their employees and/or unions.

INDEX